eat,
drink
&
remarry

Also by Margo Howard

Eppie: The Story of Ann Landers

A Life in Letters:
Ann Landers' Letters to Her Only Child

eat, drink & remarry

CONFESSIONS OF A SERIAL WIFE

margo howard

eat, drink & remarry

ISBN-13: 978-0-373-89304-1

Part of Chapter 7 appeared in the *New York Times* on April 9, 2006. Reprinted here with permission.

Library of Congress Cataloging-in-Publication Data
Howard, Margo, 1940-
  Eat, drink and remarry : confessions of a serial wife / Margo Howard.
    pages cm
  ISBN 978-0-373-89304-1 (hardback : alkaline paper)
1. Howard, Margo, 1940- 2. Howard, Margo, 1940—Relations with men. 3. Howard, Margo, 1940—Marriage. 4. Advice columnists—United States–Biography. 5. Women journalists—United States—Biography. 6. Wives—United States—Biography. 7 Remarried people—United States—Biography. 8. Divorce—United States. 9. Man-woman relationships—United States. 10. Landers, Ann–Family. I. Title.
  PN4874.H687A3 2014
  070.4'44092—dc23
  [B]
              2014006411

www.Harlequin.com

Printed in U.S.A.

For Dr. Perfect

and

ATC and ACH

"Don't go back; go on."

—*Stella Adler*

PROLOGUE

It was clearly my destiny: never a bridesmaid, always a bride. Without giving it much thought, I followed the same path as most women of my generation—the one leading straight to the altar. Granted, some of my contemporaries also had careers or grad school on their to-do list, but *pas moi.* I was neither inclined nor equipped to go to work or, perish the thought, extend my stay in academia. My focus was entirely on marriage because, to my mind, that is what you did after college. I just never dreamed I would do it four times.

I was an unlikely candidate to rack up a quartet of husbands. Mine was the life of a "privileged" (formerly known as rich), beloved only child who grew up in a stable home. My parents provided a shining example of a supportive and loving marriage. Further good fortune: my mother became Ann Landers when I was 15, so until then I had her all to myself, as it were, and in no way suffered the short shrift or long shadow that can befall a celebrity's child.

One result of being a rice-scarred veteran is that I am no longer judgmental about divorce, something many people consider a public failure. As Ann Patchett wrote, "Divorce is in the machine now, like love and birth and death." I do not deem untying the knot to be a woeful misfortune so much as an error of judgment that can be corrected, and sometimes the best fix is to simply head for the exit. To my way of thinking, divorce is not necessarily a bad thing; it can actually be a blessing, as happily remarried couples will tell you. In addition to offering an opportunity to unwind from various dysfunctions, my divorces have each led to fresh starts, renewed hope, and an extensive collection of wedding rings—only one of which resides at the bottom of a pond at 1650 Green Bay Road in Lake Forest, Illinois. Another valuable upside to my sequential marriages was expanded horizons, since each husband brought me into his world, and these spheres were very different from one another.

The motto of my small, eccentric high school in Chicago (Francis W. Parker) now seems prophetic: "We Learn by Doing."

CHAPTER ONE

*Wherein I precipitously decide
I am going to get married because . . .
why not?*

Washington, D.C., 1960

I was twenty years old. It was the summer between my junior and senior years at Brandeis University in Waltham, Massachusetts. During this three-month interval, I planned to kill many birds with one stone. I would live independently of my parents, but not in a dorm. I would have a ringside seat to participatory democracy as a worker bee in the hive of the U.S. Senate. And I would be in a brand-new dating pool! I was about to begin a summer internship for Minnesota Senator Hubert H. Humphrey who, at that moment, was running against John F. Kennedy for the Democratic presidential nomination. Humphrey was best known for being liberal and loquacious. Like Gene McCarthy and Fritz Mondale, he came from the Minnesota Democratic–Farmer–Labor Party. Having known Hubert from the time I was a kid in Wisconsin (because Mother was chairman of the Eau Claire County Democratic Party), I wanted to pitch in and be part of the campaign. And did I mention the new dating pool?

Mother had arranged for me to stay with the Stolars, close family friends who lived in Washington. Bob Stolar had been in our lives from the time I was three years old when we lived in New Orleans. He was a renowned dermatologist who pioneered the treatment of vitiligo, and he was one of the few American experts on leprosy. He was also a psychiatrist, being early in making the connection between skin eruptions and emotions. Mother had met him while volunteering at the naval hospital where he was chief of dermatology. They had struck up a friendship, and over time he would become an informal advisor/shrink to Mother, Father, and me. It was he who encouraged my mother to ditch the twin act and carve out her own identity. (Alas, the twin saw to it that this effort was not entirely successful, choosing to piggyback Ann Landers's popularity to become Dear Abby.) I had seen a great deal of "Uncle Bob" during seven years of summer camp in Maryland because he had been the medical director who came up on weekends.

He married his wife, Frances, when they were both well into their forties. She was a prim Southern schoolteacher, the archetypal spinster. They would function *in loco parentis*, as they say in Latin—and Frances may have actually been *loco*, as they say in Spanish. Frances likely had what we would today call "mood swings." She was convinced that Bob and my mother had to be sleeping together because they talked so much on the phone, and when I was their extended-stay houseguest that summer of 1960, she was convinced that Bob was sleeping with *me*! The situation was manageable, however, and there were only a few outbursts from Frances. Bob was somewhat peculiar himself, perhaps owing to his genius IQ of 200. Quite tall, he looked owlish in his large glasses, and he spoke *very* slowly. Every day he wore black leather clodhoppers built for comfort, not style—what were then called "space shoes."

Their two-story house was unlike any residence I had ever seen. It was indifferently decorated and clean but had major "collections," often to the ceiling, of *National Geographic* magazines and medical journals. The place was cluttered beyond belief. The word had no currency then, but today all that stuff would surely qualify these people as hoarders. Happily, neatnik that I was, I spent very little time at the house, as I was working during the day and out most evenings.

Although my job for Humphrey was essentially scut work, I felt like a cog in a very important wheel. This was the nation's capitol, after all. And I was also on the lookout for smart, interesting men…preferably Democrats, having been more effectively indoctrinated by my mother than my father, who was a Republican. My intern duties, in the beginning, were typically to get coffee and Danish for the staff from the cafeteria each morning, man the reception desk phone at lunch, and ride the subway in the basement to deliver folders of documents either to the House or the Capitol. (This "train" was like a string of linked golf carts on a track.) I spent a fair amount of time filing, something I had never done before. This task struck me as no more difficult than it was interesting—which is to say, not at all. As it turned out, however, I managed to make a bit of a mess of it, filing Christmas-related mail under "X" (for "Xmas") and making other idiosyncratic choices that made it challenging for people to find what they needed. When Hubert was eliminated at the Democratic National Convention in mid-July, he returned to the office and said jocularly, "It's Margo's fault. She loused up the filing system."

The "Senators Only" private elevator was very close to Hubert's office, so I started using that when I didn't feel like walking down the long hall to the public elevators. Since no one ever said to me, "What are you doing in here?" I pretty much decided I was an honorary senator whenever I needed transportation up or down. On two occasions JFK was in that elevator. Though word of his roving eye was never publicized in those days, his habits were well known on the Hill. To my great distress he did not give me a second look. Or a wink. Nothing. I felt humiliated. What was wrong with *me*? Trying to be kind, a few pals said, "He doesn't do young." That soothed my dinged ego until, years later, I read that while in the White House he sent for Mimi (an intern!) to be with him in Europe, *and she was only nineteen*. I must say that no legislative grown-ups were making passes at me—or any female intern that I knew. It is for this reason, I am certain, that the Monica Lewinksy thing threw me for a loop. I tried to imagine myself, as an intern, no less, flashing my underwear at the president of the United States (or anyone) and flirting. I could not fathom it.

For me, just being in those magisterial offices and walking those grand halls was to feel excitement. I would occasionally go to the gallery to watch proceedings on the Senate floor. Important stuff was going on down there, even if I didn't know exactly what it was. I was working pro bono, of course, as kind of a living, breathing campaign contribution. My parents provided the equivalent of a modest salary to underwrite transportation, lunches and, of course, the beauty salon. I was treated more as a friend than an employee by Hubert. He would sometimes take me with him for lunch in the senators' private dining room. His lunch companions who made an impression on me were Wayne Morse (famous for getting kicked in the head by a horse), Henry M. "Scoop" Jackson, and George Smathers (boy, was he handsome).

Midway through my internship, more substantive tasks were added to my menial duties. I was, for example, elevated to serve as "constituent liaison with the Defense Department." The Department of Defense requests I dealt with were not exactly policy related—they were more along the lines of, say, a request from the director of the Minnesota State Fair for a replacement of a (deactivated) Nike missile that fell off a truck. Someone else wanted the bubble top of a fighter jet for a punch bowl. (That request was denied.) My most amusing job was answering fan letters as though I were Humphrey. These letters were in the spirit of, "I was one of the pom-pom girls at the rally in Minnetonka. Do you remember me? Anyway, I hope you win." Those of us who answered any letters over Humphrey's signature were instructed to bury our initials in the elaborate Senate letterhead...the reason being, I suppose, that if a calamitous response got out, the offender could be easily identified.

This Washington summer felt constructive and grown-up, whereas the previous summer had been all about fun. I'd gone to Harvard Summer School—for a grand total of three weeks. My timing was impeccable, because just at that juncture I was able to get a refund for most of the tuition, making me feel thrifty as I moved my act to Hyannis to be with a charming Oklahoman from Harvard Business School.

How was this possible, you ask, with two doting parents? Well, Mother had been in Russia for some weeks, making it difficult for her to keep track of my whereabouts. She had been writing her first attempt at straight journalism. Her interest, relative to her column, was finding out how everyday Russian life compared to that in the United States, how life played out for Olga and Igor. Were their problems the same as ours? Father, as usual, was wrapped up with business and traveling, and it would not have occurred to him to check up on me. (He had, by then, started Budget Rent A Car, and was traveling more than ever.) At the end of that summer, I had fudged and told them my studies had been really useful, dropping a few academic names—H. Stuart Hughes, Crane Brinton—for good measure, and I did not fess up until years later that I had escaped from Cambridge a mere twenty-one days after entering Harvard's hallowed halls.

If this sounds as though my parents gave me a wide berth and quite a bit of freedom, that is a correct assumption. I was a precocious youngster and reasonably sophisticated as a young adult. I had a pretty freewheeling existence from the time I went to college. The reasons for this, I believe, were that my parents trusted my judgment (my mother having put in a lot of time raising me) and that they were both busy people. I would say that mine had been a permissive upbringing, so by the time I went away to school, it would have been out of character for them to treat me as anything but an independent grown-up.

But during that summer in Washington, I actually felt like an independent grown-up. And that summer was the first time I met someone who I seriously thought of marrying. Three previous proposals had been nonstarters and were certainly never taken seriously by me. One came from a Chicagoan in his late thirties with whom I went out maybe half a dozen times. He was rumored to be gay and was a real fashion plate who loved to cha-cha. I was eighteen (still in high school!) when the dancing fashion plate popped the question and I, of course, declined, recognizing that while I would have given him hetero cred, I did not need someone to pick out my clothes. And I also knew I was never going to marry anybody when I was eighteen. Another suitor was a visiting sociology professor at Harvard whose work involved drug addicts and prostitutes and who was six years junior to my father. I declined that one as well, recognizing that he was too old, although that was a real romance...for a semester. The third proposal came from a man who looked good on paper in terms of profession and family—and he was handsome, to boot—but whose ardor I was unable to return. Although it was a real romance, my inner radar told me he was a little boring for the long haul, and while he was intent on marrying me (always flattering), instinct told me he was not the one.

I had been in Washington for only a week when I met the first man I knew I wanted to marry. Someone fixed me up with Newton Froelich, a young Washington lawyer. He was in his late twenties, super smart, warm, and as we moved forward, adoring. He was tweedy and studious looking, maybe because of the glasses, and he had a sweet smile. His voice cracked when he spoke, like a young Jimmy Stewart. We saw each other constantly. We went to dinner parties where he introduced me to his law partners and friends, concerts at Wolf Trap, movies, restaurants, and of course we spent time at his apartment, just the two of us. I never spent the night because of my hall monitor hosts, and because it was 1960. I (like most of my girlfriends) was not, as they say, saving myself for marriage, but it was not a topic for general discussion. And we were suspicious of the girls who made a point of discussing their virtue.

As for memorable dates, one night in particular had an undercurrent of excitement, but it had nothing to do with the romance. Newt's law firm represented a nightclub where Sammy Davis Jr. was to perform. Washington, D.C., in 1960 was seriously segregated. This club was in a white neighborhood with white clientele, so it was deemed advisable that someone from the firm be present should the club or its owners need legal counsel. It was, as we would say today, a scene. Dozens and dozens of black protesters were outside on the street and the sidewalk with placards,

and making *a lot* of noise. They could not come in to see one of
their own. Davis, whatever his personal feelings, had accepted
the gig and expressed his gratitude to the audience in the club for
being willing to deal with the commotion in order to see him. He
did a set that lasted two hours and forty-five minutes, and he did
everything ... singing, dancing, jokes, anecdotes. It was a remarkable evening.

Within two months Newt and I decided that we belonged together,
and he asked me to marry him. I was euphoric. So *this* is what it
felt like when you were really in love and could see your whole
future with one person. And I knew he was someone my parents
would approve of. His qualities made him an unquestionably
appropriate partner for me. I had "solved" the big question so
many of the young women of my generation faced: Who will be
the man that I marry?

My parents came for a visit and liked him a lot, as did the Stolars.
Both my mother and father were amenable to my announcement,
at age twenty, that Newt and I were going to get engaged—perhaps
because Mother had been twenty-one when she married Father.
Toward the end of August we planned to go to New York City to
pick out a ring. The only problem was that as the summer's end
approached, I changed my mind. I was no longer sure he was someone I could see myself with for the long haul. I couldn't put my
finger on why, but I had cooled on the whole idea. I told him as
gently as I knew how that it wasn't him, it was me, but that I couldn't
go forward. He was crestfallen, and I felt terrible that I had said
yes—and then no. And I had no good *reason* for backing out—just
the feeling that this wasn't right for me. Mother asked why, and all

I could think of to say was that his voice had begun to annoy me. Although I sensed their disappointment regarding Newt, my parents accepted my decision and did not pressure me to reconsider. I always felt they gave me the freedom to find my way and make my own mistakes.

As I know now but did not know then, a picayune complaint is never the real reason. I just couldn't get at what the real reason was, so I landed on his voice — something that had been endearing in the beginning but was now something I didn't wish to wake up to every morning. Years later, when I followed in my mother's footsteps as an advice columnist, if people wrote me about some triviality that was annoying to them, or if they said they didn't even *know* what was bothering them about the other person, I always advised making every effort to pinpoint the real issue, and then evaluate where it fit in the scheme of things. A petty thing that seems to be an irritant is actually a stand-in for a more serious disconnect. Should the real fly in the ointment remain a mystery, my advice typically was to put the relationship on ice until the feelings were clarified. Self-knowledge is an invaluable tool when selecting a partner.

What I would eventually come to understand about my relationship with Newt is that the real reason I decided to marry him and then changed my mind is because I was an impulse buyer. I was impatient, and like many twenty-somethings and their hormones, I was inclined toward instant gratification. It never occurred to me to get to know him better. A decision that is supposed to be permanent requires, if not demands, an extended version of "sleeping on it" — yet I was not willing to do this once my feelings for Newt began to cool. Later, when I would get letters about rush-job romances where things were going really fast,

I always advised the writer to ask him or herself the question my mother often asked me, "What's the hurry?" This is not a question, alas, that I ever bothered to ask or answer in the summer of 1960.

I had always just lived in the moment, and luckily (or maybe not) if the moment didn't work out, I would be given another moment. Impatience, I have come to learn, is responsible for many blunders, in all areas of life. It has been said that maturity is the ability to wait, and whoever said it was right (I think it was my mother).

There was also another probable reason for my pulling away from this lovely guy, which only occurred to me years later, and I bet it will resonate with many women: he was too nice. I was not experienced enough to value that at the time, and now I feel embarrassed to even write it.

One thing I did know, even then, was that I had not broken the engagement from fear of commitment. Rather, commitment was exactly what I was looking for. I *knew* my next step was marriage because I didn't believe there were any other options. I was not going to grad school. I had no interest in getting a job and neither did I have any qualifications. I was a liberal arts major who was not paying terribly close attention. Like so many of my contemporaries then, I really believed the only possible next step was to get married.

(At that time the country was on the cusp of the women's movement, and although I regret it now, I didn't cotton to their message then. I've spent some time over the years analyzing the reasons for distancing myself from the movement. My nonresponsiveness likely came from the fact that I didn't need them. I never felt unfairly treated because I was a woman. Actually, I found it useful—both literally and figuratively—to bat my eyelashes. My mother was living a feminist's life, to be sure, but she, too, did not wear the label. While she used her professional clout to push for the Equal Rights Amendment, at no time did she identify herself as a feminist. However, looking back, I find that my view was too narrow. Just because *I* felt I didn't need "the sisterhood" did not negate the fact that a lot of other women did. I suspect that had I been five or ten years younger when all of this was in the air, I would've been much more receptive...just as my own daughters took it as a fact of life that they would work and that they would not take any guff because of their gender.)

So in hindsight I figured out that my evaluations of suitors were visceral, not thoughtful. I passed up a few gems, most likely because I had no specific criteria. As a young woman I wasn't factoring in quality or character; it was all about instinct and all about "now." I wasn't looking for someone rich or good looking, the goal of a lot of girls, but neither was I looking for someone solid, talented, or stable—someone who, to use my mother's phrase, "would wear well." I was unwilling (unable?) to think things through or decide what was important. Emotionally, even at age twenty (a sophisticated twenty in some respects) I was still the willful child. This may have had to do with the fact that, up until then, everything had gone my way.

It took me years to learn that decisions about important things ought not be made impulsively. Granted, this sounds like something you would find stitched on a sampler, but it's amazing how many people put aside this truism and dive right into...whatever. In my own case, I had a bit of a gambler's instinct. A cautious person, at twenty, would not meet someone in June and get engaged in August. While I know people for whom this accelerated, love-at-first-sight timetable has worked, I believe they were lucky, not smart—and probably possessed greater emotional intelligence than most. Walking, not running, into marriage gives you much better odds. Under the best of circumstances, one cannot look into the future and see how two people will grow together, or not grow together—hence the number of "gray divorces" we are now seeing, the couples who part after thirty and forty years.

In my own case, I learned through Freudian analysis (which, alas, took place too late to have influenced this engagement or prevented my first marriage) that I was a bit of an excitement junkie. Not at a conscious level, certainly, but had there been a cartoon bubble over my head during that summer in Washington, it would have said: "Well, this will be fun! I think I'll get engaged and see what that's like." With age and lots of experience I have come to understand how being "in love" and "loving" are entirely different things. This distinction was crystallized for me when I became an advice columnist. I cannot tell you the number of letters I received saying, "I love him, but I am not *in* love with him." (And yes, this is most often a woman's plaint.) That phrase is far and away the one that made me want to scream, and the thing that it made me want to scream was, "Grow up, Lady!"

New York Times columnist Jane Brody astutely pointed out that a long-running "being in love" state is an impossibility—and a good thing that it's an impossibility. She wrote, "The feelings that prompt people to forget all their troubles and fly down the street with wings on their feet do not last very long, and cannot, if lovers are ever to get anything done." She cited a study by Richard E. Lucas showing that the happiness boost that occurs with marriage lasts only about two years, after which people revert to their former levels of happiness—or unhappiness. The idea of loving someone but not *being* "in love" may be the #1 American Mistake when it comes to romantic relationships. I find "settling down" to be an apt phrase.

In the recent past, when my son got married in England, I was delighted by a portion of the vicar's wedding blessing. He referenced the novel *Corelli's Mandolin* by Louis de Bernières wherein a young woman's father tells her this:

> *Love is a temporary madness, it erupts like*
> *volcanoes and then subsides. And when it subsides,*
> *you have to make a decision. You have to work*
> *out whether your roots have so entwined together*
> *that it is inconceivable that you should ever*
> *part. Because this is what love is. Love is not*
> *breathlessness, it is not excitement, it is not the*
> *promulgation of promises of eternal passion, it*
> *is not a desire to mate every second of the day,*
> *it is not lying awake at night imagining that he is*
> *kissing every cranny of your body. No, don't blush,*
> *I am telling you some truths. That is just being in*
> *love, which any fool can do. Love itself is what is*
> *left over when being in love has burned away,*
> *and this is both an art and a fortunate accident.*
> *The reality is that love burns like a furnace for*
> *a while, but then settles, and then it has to be*
> *worked at. The romantic and sexual love described*
> *in The Song of Solomon has to grow up, to be*
> *adult. There is no future in being "in love." What*
> *you need is the strength and wisdom to go beyond*
> *being in love to loving.*

How wonderful to hear a learned man confirm that being "in love" is unsustainable. Amen to that.

And then there was my mother's famous and oft-quoted definition of love, to which, alas, I paid no attention:

> *Love is friendship that has caught fire. It is quiet*
> *understanding, mutual confidence, sharing and*
> *forgiving. It is loyalty through good and bad times.*
> *It settles for less than perfection and makes*
> *allowances for human weaknesses.*
>
> *Love is content with the present, it hopes for the*
> *future and it doesn't brood over the past. It's the*
> *day-in and day-out chronicle of irritations, problems,*
> *compromises, small disappointments, big victories,*
> *and working toward common goals.*
>
> *If you have love in your life it can make up for*
> *a great many things you lack. If you don't have*
> *it, no matter what else there is, it's not enough.*

CHAPTER TWO

Wherein I somehow — again! — make a hasty decision. Hard to believe, I know.

Later in 1960, when I returned to school for my senior year, a hall mate fixed me up on a blind date with her fiancé's cousin. This man had a purple Cadillac and not a lot of hair. He was also a smidgen shorter than I, and at five foot two, I was no Amazon. Being a bit of a brat and reading the tea leaves, I announced when I saw him that I felt the onset of a spastic colon attack and we could either bag the date or I could go and just have tea. I should not have offered him a choice because he chose to continue with the date. We wound up at Locke-Ober Café, my favorite restaurant in Boston, and I was stuck with a pot of tea. And him. Apparently he was a perceptive chap because he quickly determined this date was a twofer: the first and the last. And so it was that he suggested that his good friend John Coleman call me because Coleman was planning to move to Chicago—and I was from Chicago.

My first date with Coleman was not what anyone would call auspicious. He collected me in Waltham and basically did not talk to me for the drive into Boston which, at that time, took about 40 minutes. I made a stab at drawing him out but with little polysyllabic success. He was a freckled redhead, trim, of average height. His facial structure was sharp angles, and he was also some-what chin-deficient, which seemed rather English (which, to me, translated to being distinguished looking). Were I describing him today, I would say he looked like an unattractive Prince Charles—but I was never one of those girls particularly drawn to guys with traditional good looks.

We went to the Ritz-Carlton for dinner with a married couple he had invited and then on to the movie premiere of *West Side Story*. Interesting: a first date with a guarantee of no conversation for two hours. He also left his seat three times to smoke. (I smoked, too, then, but I never interrupted a movie to do it.) It did not register in any serious way that he was one of those people who, as Jewish grannies used to say, had "shpilkes." A fair translation would be "ants in your pants."

He asked me out again and I accepted, probably hoping he would talk this time. He did. On our second date, I found out he was five years older than I and that he was working at Tucker Anthony & R.L. Day in Boston, learning the investment banking ropes. He did mention that, starting in the sixth grade, he was reading *Barron's*. He'd gone to prep school and then to college at Rutgers. After graduating he went to Harvard Business School—but dropped out during his first semester, deciding that he knew more than they did. The drama of his life was that he was adopted. Everyone in his family knew, but *he* did not find out until age twenty, when he went to city hall for a passport. Perhaps this situation, both traumatic and angering, contributed to his chilliness.

He was, however, showering me with attention and wanted to get together every night. This I could not do, but we did have four dates within a week and a half. Things moved fast, and I was strangely drawn to him, perhaps because he was such a controlled personality, and I couldn't help but embark on the unconscious challenge "to get through to him" (making me, I guess, one of those icebreaker ships and him the iceberg).

On the fourth date he told me he was madly in love with me and asked me to marry him. Reader, I said yes. Do not ask me why because I could not tell you. It was then that he told me he had a minor bit of business to take care of: he needed to get a divorce. A *what*? Where was she, I asked? Was he dating even though he was still married? Well, he explained, they'd been separated for much of their two-year marriage, and he had not planned to rush into a divorce, but now, of course, his plans had changed. I accepted his explanation and went along with the engagement. I really do not know what possessed me. I'd had a romantic history of boyfriends who were smitten with me, warm and devoted. All I can figure out, in retrospect, is that his *very* different kind of personality was somewhere between a change and a challenge for me, and I was intrigued. A rare tribute, perhaps, to be chosen by a man who seemed so aloof, but loved *me*? His personality exhibited characteristics I had never experienced in a romance before. He was introverted and remote, the classic loner. And he was driven. There was something of a wounded soul about him that called out to me. It was as though he needed me. Think Jay Gatsby if he found Florence Nightingale (and not Daisy Buchanan).

I now believe I misread his chilliness as mystery, and his "I need not conform" attitude as power. I realize that he may have been my "bad boy," even though I did not know at the time that subliminally implied danger could serve as an attraction. Many years later I would learn—firsthand, as well as from girlfriends and my work—that bad boys were sometimes irresistible. Had I been objectively evaluating what I'd been observing in John Coleman, I would have seen that this was a man "practically woven out of red flags," to borrow critic Emily Nussbaum's perfect phrase. But I was blind to these red flags at the time. For instance, I failed to process the information that on some occasions we would wind up at his apartment and he'd pass out. He was a big drinker, which was nothing I'd ever experienced with anyone I had dated. But I ignored it.

This brings us to an aspect of human behavior that informs many facets of life, and very often romance: self-deception. We don't know what we don't want to know. An emotional decision can often override good sense because, in essence, your mind is already made up. On a wholly unconscious level I discounted this flashing warning light because I'd decided to go on this adventure with someone who was certainly "different," and therefore I blocked off any examination that would have proven me wrong. Had I been less determined, I would've taken more time and entertained the negatives. Any acknowledgment of uncertainty would have propelled me to seek counsel—doubt being one of the key motivators for people to ask the advice of others, whether it be therapists, advice columnists or friends. And in my case, a great resource was a phone call away, and it would have begun "Hi, Mom."

With no inclination to talk this decision through—with my mother or anyone else—the day after I said yes to Coleman, I called Mother to announce that he had proposed and that I had accepted and was very excited. I told her all about him, making the minuses sound like pluses—not to fool her but simply to pass on to her what I had told myself, totally unaware of what I was doing. The chilly, remote attitude of a loner, in the telling, became Yankee reserve. The noncommunicativeness morphed into his being a good listener. I translated his single-minded drive to succeed as healthy ambition. Of course I did not mention his alcohol intake, having convinced myself it didn't mean anything and would probably taper off, and also because my mother was a teetotaler whom my father called "Carrie Nation." (More fodder for Dr. Freud: many years later both Mother and I figured out that Father was a high-functioning alcoholic. He always had a Scotch in his hand, but his personality didn't change, and drinking did not stop him from successfully running a huge corporation.)

Hearing my news, Mother said the four of us should definitely get together in New York so my parents could meet Mr. Wonderful. A month later we all rendezvoused at the St. Regis. Wanting "to meet him" of course translated to "look him over." Look him over they did. Win them over he did not. Clearly having magical powers of perception, they both told me that going forward with this man would be a colossal mistake. They found his personality odd and thought he was a drinker. I ignored this. After all, it was my life, my choice. I was shocked at the resistance, however.

Some weeks later Father told me he had run a "Proudfoot" on my intended. Today they call themselves a "financial performance company," but in the early 1960s they had a division that functioned as a financial detective agency. Father gave me an abbreviated summary of their findings: "His previous wife was rich, too." Highly offended, I said, "So?" I would never be rich. My parents had always told me they were leaving their money to charity, lest it complicate my life.

Actually, twenty years later, Mother told me this, of course, was not true, but they wanted me to think it was—and perhaps make it known to any potential suitors. I really did believe it, though, imagining that everything was going to, well, I don't know, Radio Free Europe and The Humane Society. I was just unconscious enough not to work out that my father, the founder of Budget Rent A Car, might be thought of by others as rich and well connected, or that my mother's fame carried with it anything other than grateful readers. The fact that she'd been voted "Most Influential Woman in the World" one year went right over my head. (I actually remember her sending me the newspaper clipping about the honor with this note: "Now will you listen to me? Love, Mother.")

So then the campaign began. Both of my parents actually cried/begged/offered bribes to try to convince me to reverse my decision. Friends were politely unenthusiastic. But no dice. To say this universal raspberry was falling on deaf ears would have been the understatement of the year. Alas, the unanimous negative response to him meant absolutely nothing to me. When you marry anyone, I told myself, you are making a bet. Granted, some bets are more thoughtful than others, but luck is always a big factor regardless. My bet was clearly one made in the spur of the moment, and only time would reveal that some pastel masochistic propensities were dressing themselves up as Lady Luck. At this time, I felt my bet was a good one.

After many years of life experiences granting me distance from Coleman, not to mention many years of my reader mail, I now understand that a Greek chorus saying, "Don't do this" should not be disregarded. If I knew then what I know now, as they say, the question I would've asked myself is, *Why would your friends and family go out on a limb to tell you that this was a bum choice, taking the risk of becoming persona not grata?* Oh, if only I could have understood this then and *listened* to their objections, but I don't know too many twenty-one-year-olds who could be dissuaded from making a decision that they felt was theirs alone to make. (And this is the reason I know so many people who've had "a brief first marriage.") Consider the old chestnut, "Young people know everything"—and then recall the joke, "The older I get, the smarter my parents become."

Much to their credit, when I proved to be adamant about the engagement, my parents accepted the situation and went forward with a remarkable version of "let's pretend." Mother wanted a fabulous wedding for me, and Father took "Red" (his nickname for Coleman, not mine) under his wing and tried to treat him like a son. Of course a wedding required planning, which meant my leaving Brandeis after the first semester of my senior year. For me, this was no great tragedy because I didn't have the credits to graduate anyway. And, in fact, I had never planned to graduate because I hadn't planned to *be* anything for which you needed a degree. Actually, I hadn't planned to "be" anything, period. I had, up until that point, however, maintained the fiction that I was a serious student so that my parents would feel good. It was, therefore, a punch in the gut when Abe Sachar, then-president of Brandeis, wrote them a buck-up letter saying he hoped they didn't feel bad about my leaving school early because I was "the loveliest ornament they'd ever had." Oh, God, an "ornament," yet. In any event, when my Brandeis pals were beginning their second semester I returned to Chicago with a three-carat solitaire and a fiancé my parents positively loathed.

May 13, 1962
Here comes the bride; and her dad; and a battery of photographers from the wire services, all four Chicago papers, plus the photographer

that my family actually paid to be there. When Father and I started to walk down the aisle, I was so rattled by all the popping flashbulbs that when we got to the chuppah where he would "give me away" I said, "Goodbye," whereas I had planned to say, "Thank you." Then we both got teary.

Our 350 wedding guests were in the Ambassador Hotel ballroom, sitting in little gilded chairs amongst 1,600 azalea plants and masses of white roses. I wore a demure Priscilla of Boston lace gown with seed pearls. The veil was anchored by a crown. (I would love a do-over on that one.) Many luminaries were in attendance — Mother's and Father's associates from business, politics and publishing, along with friends from all over the country. Numerous friends of mine were there as well, both from Chicago and the East Coast. The groom did not have many friends there — or anywhere, for that matter. Even the best man was not exactly a friend: he was the lawyer who'd gotten Coleman the divorce from his first wife so that he could marry me.

There were two rabbis officiating, which was decidedly odd for a bride and groom who, along with their families, were not observant. Mother said we had to have the rabbi from the famously Reformed Temple we belonged to (Temple Shalom, also known as the "Church on the Lake") because it would be insulting if he were not there. The "real" rabbi was Julian Feibelman from New Orleans, where we'd lived when I was three. Mother felt a bond with him from all those years ago, perhaps because he was wonderfully eloquent and warm.

It was a very "ooh-la-la" wedding. Mother and I made all the choices together, and the wedding planner was Weddings, Inc. (The name reminded me of Murder, Inc., and I would remember that later when I realized the marriage needed to end.)

Years later, I would learn from my friends who were at the wedding that they were asking each other at their dinner tables, "Why?" Then they all turned to divination, deciding, "This will never last." The "why" question, of course, had already been asked by my parents—and ignored. Strangely, it was a difficult question to answer, even for me.

Trying to decode the thinking behind my disastrous decision years after the fact, I could never quite figure out what I had been doing or why exactly I had done it, but I was pretty sure about what I was *not* doing. I was *not* rebelling. My relationship with my loving and permissive parents was as good as any I knew of. I was not looking for a husband so I could "get out of the house." And Coleman certainly had not been the only candidate. What should have occurred to me (but had not at the time) was a favorite saying of my mother's: "Women are not reform schools." While I don't believe I had ever consciously thought that I could "fix" him—make him charming, outgoing, and a moderate drinker—I must have felt that love and I could smooth out his personality. I do believe that many women (and I suppose some men) naively believe that love and marriage will "solve" whatever problems exist. Wrong. It is wise, if not imperative, to accept and understand that *what you see is what you get*. There will be no major changes in people who are old enough to ask you to marry them.

For our honeymoon we went to Spain and Portugal, a gift from my parents. (They went to London to recuperate.) I will say this for Coleman: he had it in him to be a good sport. I remember a dinner at the Jockey Club in Madrid, a place unknown to me but not to him. Because it was a pricey place, I was surprised and excited to see beluga caviar, my fave, at bargain prices! I had, however, apparently confused grams with pesos, and mistakenly converted ounces to money (or something weird), and the ounce and a half of caviar I ordered came to $150 American dollars! (This was 1962.)

Most of our honeymoon was spent at the Son Vida Castle in Majorca. This 13th-century palace had been converted to a luxury hotel only the year before. Despite the fact that I was honeymooning with my new husband, what I remember most fondly about that stay was meeting a man at the pool. He was graying, probably in his late fifties, and he was the handsomest man I had ever seen—if you don't count Peter O'Toole. We started talking, and I found him endlessly fascinating. He was Persian and from one of the ridiculously small number (likely less than one hundred) of rich families there. This extremely attractive gentleman ran the shah's oil interests, and he was one of 49 children! I astutely guessed that he and these siblings were not all from one mother. Because they were mega-rich, those kids had been educated at prep schools in Europe and Switzerland and then went on to American colleges at the level of Harvard, Yale and Stanford. I no longer remember specifics, but *dozens* of them were high achievers. I had never heard of anything like it, most probably because I'd never heard of anyone who was one of 49 children. Would it be rude to say that talking with this man was the highlight of my honeymoon?

There just didn't seem to be a lot to talk about with Coleman. I thought it may have been that I had already heard everything he had to say in his push to get me to marry him. He was, let us say, taciturn, and marriage had not loosened him up. I admit I had expected it to, assuming that being married to me—someone he absolutely *had* to have—would miraculously make me a confidante, privy to his innermost thoughts, fears, difficulties, hopes and plans. Or how about just shooting the breeze? The only thing I did learn for certain was that he wanted to be rich. While his parents were comfortable, they lived simply. Having gone to prep school, however, he encountered boys who came from serious money—and he'd made it his life's goal to be like them.

What saved the day in Majorca was meeting another honeymooning couple, Sam and Lila Bader, with whom we would dine. Most evenings ended here as they had in Boston: my new husband would imbibe before and during dinner and then enjoy a few postprandial brandies, causing him to...fall asleep. I must say we were sexually in sync, though it was more often the sun than the moon that peeped through the draperies when we got cozy. It was, no doubt, for people like him that they wrote the song, "Love in the Afternoon."

When we returned to Chicago, we moved into Coleman's one-bedroom apartment at the Carriage House, a good Near North Side building not far from my parents. I began what I imagined to be grown-up married life. I wrote my thank-you notes. I returned thirty-two pieces of Steuben glass for credit, keeping four. I was awash in sterling silver goblets, chargers, serving pieces and *everything* I had registered for. Those 350 guests had been awfully generous. Hubert and Muriel Humphrey gave us crystal highball glasses etched with his name and the Senate logo, which I still have. The Humphreys sent me wedding gifts *three times*!

To my astonishment, I soon learned I was pregnant. I had conceived in Spain. Ole! As I mentioned previously, the early

1960s marked a time that was just on the cusp of the women's movement, and so it was still an accepted fact of life (at least in my group) that newly married young women did not particularly think about whether or not to have children. We just had them because that's what you did—you got married and had a family. For this reason there had been no thought of birth control. I was just going to leave it to fate. I wanted to be surprised. And I *was* surprised.

I had an easy pregnancy: no morning sickness, no nothing. My doctor said I was getting through this like a peasant—in the good way. I felt fine and looked rather glam. Going out in the evening I didn't even need maternity clothes. Great good luck, there was a designer at that time, Norman Norell, whose signature style was the tent dress! The labor, however (more than 30 hours) must have been karmic payback for the trouble-free run-up to the actual birth. The drugs made me profane with the nurses, and the pain had me making a great deal of noise. Not to mention I was starting to have serious doubts about those Chinese women I'd heard about giving birth in the rice fields.

Our baby was a girl, and we named her Abra, which means "breeze" in Greek. We were not, however, Greek. We were Jewish, and traditionally Jews name their children after family members who have passed away, and my mother strongly encouraged me to name my first child after *both* of her parents: Abraham and Rebecca. Abra was darling, born with a full head of dark hair that seemed to be pre-styled into a pixie cut. And best of all, she had a sunny disposition and a good-natured, placid temperament.

Oh how times have changed. Today a mother is lucky to be allowed to stay overnight in the hospital after delivery, but in those days we stayed for six days. A nurse would bring the baby in periodically to visit and nurse. I was not very good at nursing, and supplemental feedings were required. This played into my fears that I might not be maternal enough and wouldn't know what to do. I had no siblings and hadn't really spent any time around small children. Also, Coleman was only mildly interested, so it felt as though it were up to me, alone, to look after the baby. Mother, though supportive and thrilled with her first grandchild, was no help in this department, not remembering much about infant care, it being 23 years behind her. Strangely, it was my father who took on the traditional grandmother role. He did not really know what to do, but he was wild about that kid, and it was his joy to spend time with her. I believe, not wishing to offend her, he would carry her around with no diaper or burp cloth on his shoulder, allowing her to spit up on his bespoke suits. While my mother announced she was not available for babysitting, decreeing, "Children are for young people," my father, however, said we could call anytime. (Easy for him to say—he traveled a great deal. But it's the thought that counts.) And he sent Abra roses every month for a year and a half.

Being scared stiff about caring for this tiny person, I hired a baby nurse some of my girlfriends had employed, a lovely woman named Kelly. I had such a fear of being alone with Abra and doing something wrong that I begged (well, okay, bribed) Kelly not to take off the one day a week she was promised. As the three-month period we'd engaged her for neared an end, I realized I hadn't been paying much attention to what she had done to care for Abra, and I still needed her to give me lessons in how to do this mothering thing myself. Then she left us to go on to the next baby and frightened mother. Happily, Abra was a really good baby. Somehow sensing that I was a late sleeper, she would wake up, play in her crib, and not make a peep until I came in to say hello. I was particularly grateful for this on the morning of her first New Year's Day, when she was eleven months old. I awoke at 10:30 a.m. and went into her room to find that wonderful, accommodating child playing in her crib and flashing me a big smile. The kid must have somehow known about New Year's Eve.

Once Kelly departed, I was able to manage all the standard tasks involved in caring for a child. I walked Abra in her buggy, visited with other mothers, fed and bathed her. Coleman would occasionally change a diaper, which at the time I thought was heroic. All the while, though, I was wishing I could be doing something else, even if it were just reading a book. And I have realized over the years that I missed out on a lot by not focusing on my children when they were young. (I went on to have two more with Mr. Coleman.) In fact, being somewhat detached when my kids were little is the real regret of my life. Of course I have no way of knowing, but I've always wondered if I had married a warm, loving man who was crazy about kids if I might have been a different — and better—mother. My younger two children seem to have some understanding of these early difficulties of mine and have forgiven me. The eldest, Abra, I feel has not—although it was she who had the most attention from me for the first three years of her life when she was an only child.

I do not think difficult marriages, per se, make people deficient in the parenting department. In fact, sometimes a less than ideal situation can call up the better angels of one or both parents. This dedication probably springs from a stew of guilt, compensatory instincts, and just plain joy in watching one's children blossom. That said, Father Theodore Hesburgh (the longest serving president of Notre Dame, and a good family friend) said the best gift you can give children is two parents who love each other, and I think he was right. My hasty choice of a husband, alas, took a toll on the children. Coleman and I were simply playing house—and not at all well, at that.

Coleman was a like a combination of Jay Gatsby and Sammy Glick. Business, wealth, and Being Somebody were his raison d'etre. This was not as foreign to me as it might have been to someone else because my father was all about business. There was a major difference, however. Father was crazy about Mother and me, and he was warm and loving. Coleman was not. I figured out very early in the marriage that this relationship was not like the one I had grown up seeing between my parents, and this marriage did not feel wonderful. My spouse was somewhere between being a silent partner and a sparring partner.

I felt alone and I *was* alone. Coleman traveled, and when he was home the phone was glued to his ear. I realized I felt calmer and less on edge when he was gone. Whatever flaws are possible in a man relative to his marriage (excluding impotence), he had. I do not say this to be insulting but to be accurate. His word was no good, he was closed off, uncommunicative, cold, alcoholic, preoccupied and, I would come to learn, unfaithful. If I had to find a plus side, it would be that he made no particular demands on me, and he never questioned my expenditures or my need for household help.

After Abra, I wanted a second child, even though the marriage was not stellar. I had loved being an only child, yet it seemed like the thing to do was give Abra a sibling. My next pregnancy was not as easily accomplished as my first. I tried for more than two years, and when Abra was three, Adam was born. He was certainly fully cooked when he appeared, weighing 8.5 pounds and looking as though he'd been here for a while. This time the baby nurse stayed for more than a year. Though Adam was chubby and adorable, I suspect my increasing unhappiness with my marriage colored my choice to have little to do with his physical care.

As our family expanded we needed more room, so we moved to a new development called Lake Meadows on the Near South Side. Leaving the Near North area felt like going to a whole different town, as I had lived on the Gold Coast since I was fourteen. This group of new buildings had been built by an insurance company, with only one of the buildings being considered luxury residences; the rest designed for middle-class housing. We were on the penthouse floor of the luxury building with a few other young families who would become friends—and company—for me. We were there just a year and a half when Coleman decided it was time to own, rather than rent, and we moved back to the Near North when he bought us a townhouse on Astor Street from Henry Marcus, the owner of Mogen David Wines. It tickled me that there was a temperature-controlled wine cellar in the basement, and it was there that they kept their kosher wine, none of which sold for more than a few dollars a bottle.

This four-story house at 1541 N. Astor Street had an elevator, and while I always took the stairs myself, I did send the diapers up and down in the elevator. This was pretty tony real estate for a 26-year-old with two small children, but it didn't overwhelm me because of the way I had grown up, and also because I had help—both with the children and the house. Ours was the second house on that block, and next to us was the Swift mansion. Across the street was the residence of the Archbishop of Chicago. Abra marveled at the "men in black nightgowns" she'd see coming and going from the spacious yard behind the black iron fence.

(The Cardinal, at that time, John Cardinal Cody, was nicknamed "Louisiana Fats," having come from New Orleans. It would come out years later that he had most likely fathered a child with his secretary—a rare occurrence at the time at least that people knew about.

Things were going swimmingly for Coleman financially, and I had carte blanche to buy whatever I wanted. And I did. Though the term was unknown at the time, I was engaging in retail therapy. I only learned this much later, but for unhappy women shopping accomplished two things: it was about getting "stuff" and getting even. I was never what you would call a shopper, and not a big fan of hanging out in stores, unlike some girls of my acquaintance who knew all the inventory on Michigan Avenue. I had my own saleswoman at Stanley Korshak, and as they say today, "she would dress me." I would wander into Korshak's only when "Miss Diane" would phone to say a few things came in that looked like they were well suited to me. Whatever I liked, I bought. I did not buy jewelry for myself; that always came from Coleman. I furnished the house, of course, and shopped for the children. This was a continuation of the pattern of my youth: money was no object. This, of course, was communicated to the children, which turned out not to be a good thing. As they advanced from the toddler stage, even I knew it was unattractive for children to be asking, "What are we taking today—the Mercedes or the Rolls?"

Money was an integral part of the dynamic between Coleman and me and also between Coleman and the children. With me, I believe Coleman's financial open-handedness was meant to keep me quiet or keep me happy. With the children, getting them whatever material things they wanted was actually an attempt to buy them off. Like many successful men for whom spending time with their children is not paramount, *things* were a substitute for time. For one of Adam's birthdays, Coleman's present was for our houseman to take Adam to a hockey game.

The situation between us was periodically painful (or at least it was for me; I don't know if he noticed). I was in denial of the obvious and would repeatedly resolve to give it another go—not yet willing to throw in the towel. In the mid-1960s divorce was not all that common amongst young couples I knew, and I didn't want to admit to making an error of such magnitude. I also did not have my own resources and assumed I probably never would—because, as I mentioned before, I assumed that my parents had stipulated that their wealth eventually go to Radio Free Europe or the Humane Society.

I did not know much about Coleman's business except that we spent an awful lot of time with bankers and business people. Did I mention he was not very communicative? When Abra was young, a business reporter asked if she knew what her father did. "Yes," she said. "He owns things." And that's about all I knew. One element of his good fortune—and his actual fortune—was that, when we married, my father introduced him to his bankers and probably offered guarantees, and both my parents used their connections on his behalf. It was well known in town that he was Eppie and Jules Lederer's son-in-law. I have always felt that being so driven, he would have become rich without us, but it probably would have taken longer.

It dawned on me later that I was a trophy wife for Coleman, though this was before anyone used the term. It also dawned on me *much* later that my being the yin to his yang was the reason for his being such an ardent suitor. I was his total social opposite. I say this with no modesty, false or otherwise: I was charming, funny, a good conversationalist—and I was sober. I was also, then, good-looking and stylish. It is very hard to admit, and I couldn't for years, but his pursuit of me probably had more to do with business and connections than with love.

To be fair, there were a few people, here and there, who did not find me so charming. This had to do with a lifelong trait of mine which Father called "mouth on a trolley." I was basically given to saying what I was thinking. I have an extensive history of ill-advised, articulated observations, one of which will give you the flavor of the younger, less thoughtful me.

We had been asked by one of Coleman's bankers to invite some new Astor Street neighbors to dinner. This couple owned a bank in Miami and had recently moved to Chicago. They were older than we, and the wife was on the flashy side, with Lucille Ball red-orange hair and a tiny, surgeon-sculpted nose. After dinner they invited us to their place for a brandy. We were in the paneled library where, over the fireplace, was an oil portrait of a woman who resembled Lady Bird Johnson if she'd been a redhead. "Who is that?" I asked. The wife said, "Well, that's me." Honest to God the next thing out of my mouth was, "No! Who would have a portrait of themselves with their old nose?" We were, and this is no exaggeration, shown the door three minutes later and the evening was over. (But seriously, who would not get a new portrait?)

Ours was definitely an "opposites attract" situation, though without the underpinnings for compatibility. Such a dynamic can work when a couple's differences and deficiencies can be balanced in complementary ways. But we did not have that. My life was not happy and I was in no way content, though no one knew this except my parents. I did not confide in friends, feeling it would be awkward, if not shameful, to whine about Coleman's inadequacies without having made the decision to do something about it. My reluctance to fix what was broken—one way or the other—manifested itself in shopping, being a lady who lunched and involving myself with charities. And I did the best I could in my role as a mother, which I am the first to admit was none too good. In an emotional sense, it was as though I were "keeping two sets of books," to borrow a wonderfully expressive phrase from Christopher Hitchens. My public self and private difficulties were quite far apart, which of course took its toll. I was somaticizing, which for me meant stomach problems.

There wasn't a great deal of outward fighting. Silence and pretense prevailed over arguing because, when he was challenged, I found him so harsh and scary that I often made the choice just to let things ride. And when we did get into it, there was something about his anger and frigidity that took away my ability to think clearly and fire back. Later, I would hear of this odd phenomenon from a number of women who wrote to me seeking advice. There are certain people who, from a sense of power—real or imagined—believe that if they say something, the listener is supposed to believe it. It's not unlike a twisted version of a mother saying to her youngster, "Because I said so." Such a person in an argument is the *soi-disant* authority, and that's that. This is hard to go up against because issues can't be addressed when no one is talking about them.

For the first couple of years of the marriage, our winter vacations were spent at the Montego Bay Racquet Club in Jamaica. That was, of course, all about tennis. Coleman was good at the game but I did not play at all. I distinctly remember one year where the guests were a landlocked "Ship of Fools," people who, when I spoke of them later to friends, always elicited the remark, "You are making this up." Believe me, a novelist could not have conjured up this crowd.

There was a partner at Lehmann Brothers whose wife was obsessed with backgammon and reportedly had an equine disease being treated by a veterinarian. (Well, that's what they said.) He played at the club, though they had a house on the island. Should you be invited for lunch, there was no talking allowed because of the backgammon games. Another guest at the club was a Guinness heir who was dating a black shop clerk from downtown Montego Bay. There was a man from Baltimore who was taking a sabbatical from the United States because of tax troubles, and his traveling companions were two Lebanese belly dancers. Then there was a seven-times-married lesbian traveling with, perhaps married to, a professional gambler who had been asked by the government of Nassau to please leave because he was fleecing the tourists and it was bad for business. To my great regret I was not a writer at the time.

Although not a tennis player, I knew who some of the greats were from reading newspapers: the Panchos—Segura and Gonzales, Rod Laver (who Coleman actually resembled), Ken Rosewall, and Don Budge. Well, Budge, three-time Wimbledon winner, was the pro at the Montego Bay Racquet Club. He and his girlfriend at the time, Lori (who later became his second wife), held court (no pun intended) at their invitation-only dinner table. Coleman was too good to take lessons, but he wanted to be invited to dine at that table. So guess who was sent to the pro shop to buy tennis whites and be fitted with a racquet? This is how it turned out that I, not athletic and not interested, ended up taking tennis lessons with Don Budge—sometimes two a day.

One problem was that Budge kept a pitcher, courtside, of orange juice and gin, and he was more often schnockered than not. He was not very forgiving of my ineptitude with tennis, not to mention my lack of interest. ("I have never *seen* a backhand like that.") But the lessons did get us to The Table. And every night he would launch into recollections of Wimbledon. My goal became getting out of the lessons and out of the Don & Lori Dinner Club. One night, a new couple joined the group. Budge started in with his glory days again, and I said (of course knowing the consequences), "Oh, Don, not your Queen Mother bullshit again." We did not have to have dinner with them anymore, and my tennis lessons came to an end.

An odd footnote is that years later, when I had moved to Boston, I was invited to a dinner party, and the hostess mentioned that Don Budge would be there—Don's son was married to the hostess's daughter, and there was to be some ceremony having to do with their baby. Whether it was a christening or the Jewish equivalent I do not remember, but I felt honor bound to tell her of our history. She laughed, telling me she was well aware of his drinking, and she insisted that I come. I must say, re-meeting Budge was not what I expected. He remembered our meeting previously but, much to my relief, not my tennis game or my big mouth. A fine time was had by all.

It was during our first trip to the Racquet Club that we started playing a game we didn't *know* was a game. Coleman would misbehave more egregiously than usual (misdemeanors of the booze-fueled variety, often involving vampire hours and God knows what, or who, else) and the next morning there would be maybe $1,500 on the dresser with a note inviting me to go shopping. I later learned what we were doing from psychiatrist Eric Berne's bestselling book *Games People Play*. Ours was, "Now I've Got You, You Son of a Bitch." Couples apparently do this all the time. The dynamic is simple: someone misbehaves, the partner who's been given cause for distress is paid tribute, in whatever form, and is thereby manipulated into forgiveness. The peace offering can be a present or a promise to do better. In Berne's terms, the game of "Now I've Got You, You SOB" stipulates that the partner who has been wronged receives what the errant partner believes will smooth things over. And that is how I got some really beautiful jewelry.

This ritualized back-and-forth game of forgiveness is not healthy, of course, and only the neurotic play. Some couples keep the games going for a very long time. The smart ones, however, see a marriage counselor or a divorce lawyer.

Soon I was driving a Rolls-Royce Silver Cloud. This was not one of the Coleman Peace Prizes, it was more like a billboard on wheels advertising that the man of the house was successful. He didn't want to be thought showy by driving a Rolls himself, so he took what he believed to be the subtle route: he bought it for me. I must say it was a beautiful automobile and incredibly quiet. I was not crazy about riding so high in my mid-twenties (in both the literal and figurative sense of the word), but it was gorgeous.

On occasion, Coleman's business trips were vacations for me and one time I was parked at the Beverly Hills Hotel for a week. On that trip I made an interesting acquaintance. At that time Howard Hughes was living in a Beverly Hills hotel bungalow with his then-wife, the movie star Jean Peters. Different hotel personnel were happy to pass on this intelligence. I figured out which bungalow was his because there was always a man on the porch wearing a suit and a fedora. (This was in Southern California.) When I would walk by I'd nod, and he would nod back. One day we wound up on neighboring stools at the soda fountain—like a coffee shop in the basement of the hotel. We started to talk, and with a minimum of verbalization he confirmed that he was, in fact, working for who I thought he worked for. In the course of the conversation, he did provide a few interesting nuggets. One was that everything that came through the mail addressed to Hughes went to a warehouse, and that was the end of that. The other was that he had an interesting and quiet way of helping graduate students in engineering—his field. Every property he owned (aircraft hangars, buildings, boats) was guarded, and those sentries were mostly graduate students who could use the time to study. All of the man's eccentricities aside, that aspect of his character seemed quite sweet.

Coleman was becoming a financier to be reckoned with, though people did not particularly warm to him. Take, for instance, Jonas Salk, whose ticket to posterity was the Salk polio vaccine. I do not know if Coleman was giving him money or helping him raise it, but my husband was heavily involved with the Salk Institute for Biological Studies, and we would see Jonas both in Chicago and La Jolla. He and I hit it off from the beginning, one of our bonds being *Yiddishkeit*, another one being that he had a dry sense of humor like mine. We related to our Jewishness in the same way. Though nominally Jewish (but maybe not actually because he was adopted), Coleman did not relate to it in any way, and I always thought he would have given his left one to be Episcopalian instead. My father called him "Jewish by denial." In any case, Salk's relationship with Coleman was business; with me it was personal.

On one trip, showing us around his lab at the Institute, he said he was working on Aleutian Mink Disease.

"May I have the subjects made into a coat when you conclude the research?" I asked. He said no.

On one of our trips out west, Jonas took us to his avocado ranch, about an hour and a half drive from the lab. Not looking to spend more time with Coleman than necessary, he instructed me to travel in his car and for Coleman to follow us in the rental car. We all could've gone together, of course, being three normal-sized people, but Coleman was not known for having wide-ranging conversations in such situations.

During that ride Jonas and I talked the whole time. I loved the intellectual conversation and the ease with which we could talk. I had none of this with Coleman, and it was in situations like this that I realized how wanting my marriage was. I was particularly interested in how Jonas had been able to beat Albert Sabin to the successful polio vaccine, since Sabin had started his research first. Jonas said he instinctively knew where the answers lay, allowing him to skip several steps—although he had to go back and prove them. And it was then that I discovered that this calm, reserved man had quite an ego. I told him I thought his signal achievement with polio should have been worth a Nobel Prize. He agreed, and I shall never forget the remark that followed:

"Now I know how Galileo and Copernicus felt."

Fortunately I doubt he would have ever said anything like that in public.

From fairly early in the marriage my gut told me we would not grow old together. I toyed with the idea of cashing in my chips

at various times. That instinct manifested itself strongly one evening when Mother, Father, Coleman and I were having dinner
at The Pump Room, the legendary celebrity-studded restaurant
in The Ambassador East Hotel. "Red" said something that angered
me, and I actually started hollering at him. In The Pump Room.
In Booth #1. The next morning my mother called and suggested
that I "see someone." So at the age of twenty-four, having been
married for two years and having just one child, I began an analysis
that would last four years and would, ultimately, lead me to leave
the marriage.

Of course, professional help isn't feasible for everyone, which
is why so many people wind up looking for help from advice
columns or call-in radio shows with psychologists, or by speaking
confidentially with a family friend whose judgment they trust.
The predicament most often is about relationships. People want
validation that what they're living through is not acceptable, or
guidance to a possible remedy, or a new way of seeing the problem. And often people simply need encouragement in order to
do what they know, deep down, they must do.

I opted for Freudian analysis because that's what most people
were doing at the time. I was going four days a week, and it was
like having a job. I was lucky in that I was on the couch, literally,
where traditionally the talk is one way, but my analyst, a very
senior female doctor, wove in some strands other than Freudian,
so that she was both talking to me and with me. On a few occasions, she actually gave me advice, which is about the last thing
a strict Freudian would do.

A few years into the therapy, I started to understand the unspo-
ken message I had received from my mother growing up: I was to
be a Jewish geisha, and men (ultimately *a* man) would be the best

part of my life. This had been the upbringing *she* had had, but her inner drive and her twin sister caused her to veer away from that goal—although she tried mightily to have it both ways. Nothing was expected of me except that I be someone's wife, and then a mother. Being on the receiving end of quite a lot of male attention starting in high school served as confirmation that my mother's message was right. Also, it is apparently not uncommon for girls—at least in a first marriage—to find in their spouse a version of the dominant parent; in my case, the dominant parent was my mother. With Coleman, I had confused his seeming assurance about *everything* with the type of strength I saw exhibited in a positive way in my mother.

In time, I began to see a clear path that would lead to me living my own life. I began to understand that I didn't have to be married, and certainly not to someone with Coleman's emotional makeup. I was moving past my original, ingrained assumption that marriage was supposed to follow college, and instead I was waking up to the fact that marriage wasn't the only option. Having done that, and done it badly, I had to entertain the idea of charting a different course. With two children and a difficult, joyless husband who was a non-nurturing father in the bargain, I no longer had hope for my marriage and finally decided to leave.

Except that is not what happened. I found I was pregnant. And I could see no upside to beginning divorce proceedings while carrying a third child.

I felt stalled by this pregnancy and wished it hadn't happened, but I carried on as though I had no plans to unload a husband. It wasn't easy, and I felt like I was keeping a stressful secret. I tried to stay busy, though, which *was* easy. I could do whatever I wanted because I had good help. Coleman could pay the freight and domestic skills were not my strong suit because he could afford to pay to have help at home. This is how I rationalized abdicating to our domestic staff. Adam and Abra were being properly cared for, and the house was well run. Although the situation was far from what I'd wished for in a marriage, I felt I was doing the best that I could. And as my mother always said, "People do the best they can. No one starts out to do a half-assed job."

About two-thirds of the way through that pregnancy, we went to Boca Raton, Florida, for a couple of weeks, and during that trip I discovered that Coleman liked to play poker. Or that's what he said he was doing until two and three in the morning. "Playing poker with the guys" is a refrain I heard many times on that trip. I was not sure what guys he knew down there, but given all the things that were already wrong with our marriage, that was a mere bagatelle.

Toward the end of our stay I developed a madly annoying itch in the pubic area. I went to a local ob-gyn, thinking it might have something to do with the pregnancy. However, the doctor identified the trouble as crabs—a condition about which I was blissfully naïve. Wishing to be comforting, I am guessing because of my "condition," the doc said that while crabs/pubic lice were usually sexually transmitted, one could pick it up other ways. He asked what I did during the day. I said I didn't swim or sun, I mostly sat under an umbrella or a tree and read. That nice man said I most likely got the infestation from the tree, which I certainly did not believe. Instead I conclusively added one more flaw to the mental list I had accumulated about Coleman as a husband. I had, of course, suspected that my successful, heavy-drinking, traveling, and out-til-all-hours husband may have been running around, but until the proof was crawling around on me, I had pushed such thoughts aside—because, without actual proof, there was no point in confronting him. His approach to anything he didn't want to admit was deny, deny, deny.

To distract myself from an increasingly unhappy home life, I decided I needed a project. Politics beckoned—just as they had for Mother before she went into the newspaper business. And just when I needed it, there was a campaign waiting for me! A friend's husband was running for Illinois state treasurer. The friend was Nancy Stevenson, the charming Southern wife of Adlai Stevenson III—son of the better known Adlai Stevenson II (the eloquent two-time presidential candidate) and great-great grandson of Adlai the First who had been Grover Cleveland's vice-president. (That's what you call lineage!) Because the campaign didn't have much money, a group of Nancy's girlfriends wound up with quite a bit of power.

I worked the public relations aspects of the campaign. I chose Adlai's publicity pictures and wrote copy with an eye to countering his somewhat formal persona—which is why the image on most flyers and posters was of him walking on the beach of Lake Michigan with his jacket slung over his shoulder and his tie loosened. (Alas, we couldn't get him out of his good shoes.) And I was Nancy's speech writer...sort of. We would both write down bullet points on envelopes. We were really in the trenches and sometimes went to three teas in one day in downstate Illinois. She would speak, and the pregnant sidekick could be counted on to eat pastries at every stop. I was also Nancy's companion and driver for trips out of Chicago—except that I didn't like to drive on the highway, so she drove the driver. It was great fun. And we won.

My "campaign baby," Andrea Ted, was born on May 17, 1967, three weeks after what the doctor said would be my due date. Andrea's nurse was Thelma Jackson (who wished to be called

"Jackson"), a take-charge, smart, cheerful black woman. When she joined our household on May 23, the day we brought the tiny baby home (another daughter with a natural pixie cut!), it was she who started calling her charge "Cricket." I remember her saying, "This child is as smart as a cricket." I knew nothing of smart crickets, but the two older kids picked up the name and it stuck. Adam and Cricket were 17 months apart, not exactly Irish twins, but close enough to form a real bond, whereas Abra, having been an only child for three years, was not particularly close to the younger ones. In time, she basically designated Cricket her maid.

Jackson became important to us all and I asked if she would consider giving up being an infant nurse to stay with us. She said she'd been asked that many times and had always said no. There must have been something about Cricket, though, because at the end of three months she told me she'd reconsidered and would stay as long as we wanted her to. And she did stay with us until she died of a brain tumor, four years later. It was a great sadness for our family. Adam went into a depression, Cricket of course felt bereft, and I felt a real sense of loss. Even Coleman exhibited kindness. He visited her in the hospital and said her job would be waiting and he hoped she would return soon. To my later regret, I did not allow the children to go to her funeral with us, thinking they were too young, but I know now that it would have been a touching goodbye that would have communicated finality.

Jackson had offered me a great measure of comfort because the kids loved her, she loved them and she was an excellent manager. I felt that while I was biding my time and slogging through a rotten domestic situation, the children would at least have a stable daily life. By that time I'd also employed a houseman, mostly so Adam

would have a male figure present in a household of female domestic staff, two sisters, a mother, and a distant, often absent father. Or
as Abra told a business reporter years later, after my divorce from
Coleman, "We lived with all those crazy-ass maids and butlers."
(I never made a fuss about language with the children. All I asked
was that they not say "fuck" in front of my mother.)

Coleman was, let us say, upwardly mobile, and he started
collecting expensive art. I think he liked having dealers dance
attendance on him, and collecting offered a new and — to his
mind — elevated social entree. I frankly did not care. Art to me,
then and now, was something with which to decorate the walls,
and it had to speak to me at some level; its investment value never
interested me.

Perhaps to accommodate the art, he wanted a grander place
than the townhouse on Astor Street. We landed — with some degree
of difficulty, because the building didn't allow Jews at the time — at
2450 Lakeview in a 17-room, 9,000-square-foot apartment. It was
a 12-story building, and each family had a floor. Tish Baldrige,
who had been Jackie Kennedy's White House social secretary,
and later became an etiquette expert, was one of my neighbors.
The owner of a major real estate firm in Chicago (with his own
restricted buildings) was so frantic that a Jewish family might get
into that building that he called the chairman of the building's
board, Herman Van Mell, and offered him $25,000 more than
the asking price and said he would buy it personally to keep us
out. To his credit, Van Mell declined the offer and kept his word
to us — and there went the neighborhood. A year and a half later
I got some close Jewish friends in, and some years after that, when
I'd already left, Oprah's Jewish money manager moved in, as did
film critic Gene Siskel.

By now I was really conflicted. I wanted out of this debilitating marriage, but I had three kids under the age of five and wondered if there were not some last ditch effort I could make to keep things going and manage to stay sane. It dawned on me that maybe if I had an "afternoon friend" I would be happier. I decided—yes, I actually decided—that I would have an affair to see if that changed anything. I didn't have anyone in mind, but I would look around. How hard could it be? I considered this a therapeutic experiment, honest to God. The idea was a deliberate attempt to determine if I could stay married.

It didn't take long for me to land on someone. I was at a party when Coleman was out of town, and a good-looking married man who was not terribly bright was paying a lot of attention to me. He might as well have had a neon sign on his forehead that flashed "playboy." He was clearly a member of the Lucky Sperm Club and prototypically "The Son." His father owned a major manufacturing company in the automotive sector. We wandered into the bedroom where all the coats were and kissed a couple of times. Then he asked me to meet him the next afternoon at The Standard Club. We thought we were being awfully clever by hiding in plain sight. Whoever might see either one of us in the lobby would assume we were headed to the dining room for lunch. The club had hotel rooms, of course.

Well, my therapeutic adultery didn't exactly work out. The guy couldn't get it up. There's my answer, I thought, perhaps a sign from God...along with my realization that I didn't actually have any interest in living that way. Even as a woman younger than thirty, I wondered how (older) women I knew could live so dishonestly. My intellectual aversion to this kind of behavior was

not about guilt or morality; it just seemed that having an afternoon friend had a lot of potential potholes: discovery, disdain,
falling in love, sneaking around and the likely underlying feeling
that things *still* weren't right. My gut feeling then became my
professional opinion later: if a marriage is untenable and misery-
making, the most productive thing to do is work on getting out
of that marriage. For many women—and it was certainly true for
me—an adulterous diversion ultimately proves too complicated
and therefore unsatisfactory as a solution because nothing really
gets "solved." All you have done is introduce a different set of
problems, along with the need for secrecy. And if discovered,
there can be painful consequences compounding the problems of
a rotten marriage.

Now I was 0 for 2. Not only did I not pick a loving husband,
I couldn't even commit adultery successfully. I had one other ace
up my sleeve. Maybe if I had a job I could override the domestic
mess. I mean, I knew people in really bad marriages who basically
did a work-around by having careers. Although I was not a writer
then, I got an idea from George Plimpton, whose journalism was
all the rage. I would write a book about doing ten glamorous jobs
for women. I would do these jobs as a dilettante, for which I was
certainly qualified. From our days in Lake Meadows, I knew Arnie
and Zorine Morton. Arnie was the food and beverage manager
for the Playboy Clubs, and to the food business born. His grandfather started Morton's, the Chicago steak house. He was much
older than his wife, but they had a young child, adding to the
nursery on our floor. Because Gloria Steinem had already snuck
in as a Playboy Bunny and written about it—much to Playboy's
displeasure—I asked Arnie for permission to have that be my first
glamorous job. My pitch was that since Steinem had already done

them dirt, what more could happen to them? Arnie agreed to let me proceed.

My next step was to see if such a book was viable. The charming Oklahoman who had extracted me from Harvard summer school a decade earlier was now an investment banker at Allen & Company. We'd stayed in touch, so I called and asked if he knew any book publishers who might tell me if my idea was any good. He was well connected and arranged for me to meet with the editorial head of Random House, so I went to New York "to take a meeting." It was agreed that my idea was good, but they would have to see the writing. After seeing the Playboy Club chapter they would decide whether or not to proceed with a contract. If it were a go, my editor would be Bennett Cerf's son, Chris. Interesting, I thought... both of us young and the offspring of print celebrities. Only he was already working at Random House, and I had never written anything more substantial than a college term paper.

So off I went to make this happen. The fittings for the rabbit costume were excruciating. Those corseted Bunny outfits were somewhere between Spanx and an S & M getup—mostly the M. I could barely breathe. Luckily I had gotten my figure back after Cricket, but still. The way they made all the girls look busty was to put the cotton "tails" in the bra, with your own bosom resting on top, as it were. It was Arnie's order that I be the photo Bunny who went around the club snapping pictures, probably wisely believing that it was too dangerous to let me carry a heavy tray of drinks.

Though not quite an armed camp, things were quite frosty at home. "Dysfunctional" I believe we would call it today. On my third and last night at the Playboy Club, Coleman showed up with his newish friend, Marshall Field V. Basically they had come to make fun of me. Because Marshall's sister, Joanne, had become a friend of mine, we had enlarged our social circle. Coleman was pretty tanked up and essentially was heckling me. I was enraged. They left a couple of hours of before closing time—which was 2:00 a.m.

The comedian headlining during my three-day stint was Hank Bradford, the head writer for Johnny Carson's *Tonight Show*. After the customers left, he said I looked seriously glum and asked if I'd like to have a cup of coffee. We sat at one of the tables and I told this willing listener the drama behind my husband and his pal showing up. He was sympathetic and I was furious, and I was also grateful for someone to talk to. He asked if I wanted to come back to his hotel with him and I said yes, because I certainly wasn't interested in going home. And unlike my last endeavor, this one could get it up.

Wishing to make a statement, I stayed out until eleven the next morning, a fact that had consequences I had never dreamed of. When I hadn't come home, Coleman called the police *and* Arnie Morton. The police, of course, found neither me nor my corpse, but Arnie called me later that day, and now *he* was furious. He reminded me that I'd convinced him to let me work there to write a piece because, after Steinem, what more could happen? "Well," he was hollering into the phone, "You know what's worse than Steinem's sneaking in as Bunny and then killing us? Ann Landers's daughter disappearing from a Playboy Club!"

I wrote up my Bunny experience (minus the sleepover), and then put the piece in a drawer. This was no time to try to write a book. The act of writing, however, felt surprisingly rewarding. It was not a slog to get my thoughts on paper—in fact it was easy, which came as a surprise. My dilettante project, however, would have to wait. Like Caesar crossing the Rubicon, the die was cast. Now it was a question of when, and how.

One thing I did have in this marriage that was otherwise missing so much was occasional repartee that to me always sounded like movie dialogue. A particularly memorable event took place one night when Coleman was in the library doing desk work and drinking. There was something odd about our phone system that caused a short, muted sound to emanate from all the other phones whenever the receiver was lifted in one room. I was trying to go to sleep and heard that noise, so I picked up the phone. Hearing me pick up, Coleman ended the call he was trying to make. This happened about three times. I was now curious about whom he was trying to call. I finally succeeded without his realizing that I'd picked up and listened as the call went through. I then heard him tell *someone* that he would be arriving at the Beverly Hills Hotel around eight o'clock and would be in Bungalow (# whatever) and hoped to see her there.

"Who is this?" I said.

Coleman furiously tried punching the hook switch buttons to end the call, but because another extension had the connection, the call was not ended.

"Well, who is *this*?" asked the "someone" on the other end of the line, who sounded like a Judy Holliday clone.

"*This* is Mrs. Coleman."

"He said he was *divorced*!" she cried.

"Well, he's gonna be," I said. At which point Coleman came racing into the bedroom and said it was not what it sounded like.

"Goodnight," I said, and went to sleep.

The next day, a nice young man who worked for Coleman paid me a visit. He explained, essentially, that he was mortified, being a married man and all, but the call to the someone had been on *his* behalf, and he felt he had no choice but to confess because he did not want it to look like John was arranging a rendezvous for himself. I told him he was really nice—and loyal—to come tell me this, but I did not for one minute believe him. Coleman, by the way, was known to be murder to work for. I was not the only one in therapy because of him. His executive assistant, a wonderful woman, wound up seeing a shrink simply to keep her job and not go berserk from his machinations and unpredictable behavior.

Soon after that night, things really started to move. For a while Coleman had been coming home at five or six in the morning. I had a strong hunch he was at Joanne Field's. We had been socializing quite a bit with her and her friends, and I'd noticed two things: 1) she and Coleman seemed to have a connection that went beyond friends at a party, and 2) she could also match him drink for drink. One night at about midnight, I drove over to her apartment and—sure enough—there, parked in front of her building, was his car.

It was that confirmation that led me to contact a heavy-hitter divorce lawyer, Ben Davis. In those days, proof of adultery was the best way to get out of a marriage "advantageously." Davis felt we should engage a private investigator, and a meeting was set up at his office for me to meet the head of the agency. He was a lovely man, and I felt very comfortable with him. We talked about Coleman's traveling and Joanne's city apartment, as well as her homes in Hobe Sound, Florida, and Peterborough, New Hampshire. It was agreed that when I was certain they were together, a PI from the agency would get photographs. When I said his preferred hotel in New York was the Carlyle, the head of the agency said, in that case, because their lobby was so small, he would need to choose two preppy-looking guys so they would not look out of place and call attention to themselves. I do not know why these people traveled in pairs, but I didn't much care because, ultimately, Coleman would be paying the bill.

Now my life became a soap opera. I had to continue as if I didn't know of his affair with Joanne, and give no clue that I was lining up my ducks to end the marriage. Then one day he announced that our whole family, with Jackson, of course, was going to Hobe Sound as Jo's guests! I'll say this: the guy didn't lack *froideur*.

The strain of this mess was such that I was losing weight and down to 104 pounds. I thought I looked fabulous; Mother thought I had cancer. She did not know all the details of what was going on, but she knew some: most significantly that I was done with the marriage—just as she and my father had predicted—and was planning my exit, using Joanne as a way to get out. Jackson knew everything, both because she lived with us and because she was, in a way, a surrogate mother to me as well as the children. I told Ben Davis about the proposed Florida trip and said I didn't want to go. He encouraged me to go ahead with it, though I am not sure why, and I complied. I asked if the PIs could use this trip to my advantage. He said no, Hobe Sound was such that they couldn't even get on the island and hang around Jo's house without causing notice. This was a hellishly difficult trip for me and I actually slept with a knife under my pillow thinking (obviously being paranoid) that if they were so bold as to arrange a trip like this, why not do away with me, as well? The dynamic was clearly meant to be punitive, if not cruel. The two of them behaved as though I were not there. One thing I did pick up from this hideous trip, however, was that Jo talked a great deal about her house in Peterborough. This suggested rather pointedly that Coleman would wind up there, most likely in the near future.

Returning to Chicago, I met with Ben Davis and told him I was pretty sure my erstwhile girlfriend and my husband would soon meet up either in New York or New Hampshire. He arranged with the head of the agency to have two men in New York when I informed him that Coleman had left. If Coleman and Joanne wound up in Peterborough, two more men would join the group, and I would accompany them from Chicago. Only Jackson and my mother knew about the plan.

How was this paid for? I certainly couldn't, at this point, have the bills sent to Coleman's office, as was my habit. So I asked Mother if she would front me the money — at which point I had to tell her I was now positive he was running around and that it was with my pal, Joanne. Mother felt that direct payment from her would be unwise, so she enlisted her good friend Bob Stolar (whose house I'd stayed in during my Washington internship) to pay those bills.

Sure enough, not too long after we'd returned from Hobe Sound, Coleman announced he was going to New York on business. As I watched him pack, I noticed he threw in a few crew-neck sweaters. One seldom needs casual clothing for Wall Street so I knew he was going to Peterborough. I called Ben Davis to tell him that Coleman would soon be off to New York, and the two preppy PIs were dispatched. Then I told Ben that Coleman would go on to Peterborough, and he asked how I knew that. When

I told him it was because he packed crew-neck sweaters, he said he could not in good conscience let me spend all that money on the extra detectives based on sweaters. I remember telling him, "Ben, you ain't never been a woman, and they don't call it 'women's intuition' for nothing."

The two guys who were on Coleman's tail in New York would phone in reports to Davis, who would then phone them to me. He was seeing no women. The only thing they couldn't figure out was one meeting where Coleman's limousine rendezvoused with another on the New Jersey Turnpike. Now I was really screenwriting in my head. He was a drug dealer! He was the money manager for the mob! Why couldn't he be just a regular straying husband, like all the others?

Two days later "the boys" phoned to say they were on their way to the airport. The next call said they were at a small feeder airline. They were going to Peterborough. The New York twosome would go and check into a motel there. It was off-season, so getting a room would not be a problem. Then, arrangements were made for me to meet *my* twosome at O'Hare the next day.

I was strangely exhilarated. I wore dark glasses, feeling certain that everyone in the airport knew about my mission. The two investigators and I flew to Boston, and we then rented a car for the hour-and-a-half drive to Peterborough. Early that evening we three joined the New York duo at the motel. Having their pick of *all* the rooms, they chose one at the front so they could observe the road. Because so many places were closed, we "dined" and snacked from the machines offering candy bars, coffee, and soft drinks. The best any of us could do was to take catnaps. Believe me, you don't experience adrenaline like that until you're a woman on a mission with four private detectives.

My duo and I learned that early on that morning, the New York guys, who had made it to Peterborough by then, had observed a painter's truck that drove by about 7:00 a.m. They followed it and saw that it parked at Jo's house. But Ben had instructed us we could not force our way into the house: we must be admitted. So we brainstormed during the night, discussing how we were going to get into the house. I landed on the idea of our being a *Life* magazine crew—if questioned—making the cameras somewhat explainable. Five strangers being "welcomed" at seven in the morning, one of them with cameras hanging around his neck, posed a definite complication.

At about 6:00 a.m., I went into our communal bathroom and started putting on makeup. After I was in there for about fifteen minutes, one of the guys knocked and asked if I was alright. I said I was just fine. When I emerged they all looked at me—and one of them actually whistled. I did look quite fab—certainly for 6:30 a.m.

"What is this about?" they asked. It was remarked that this was quite unusual because most of their clients, when in similar circumstance, were weepy nervous wrecks who looked rather haggard.

"He is going to remember this morning," I said. "And a girl always wants to look her best."

To this day, I can't really fathom how I took control of the situation, but when the painter's truck drove by at 6:55 a.m., I said, "Let's go." We pulled in a few minutes after the painters and knocked on the front door.

"We've come to surprise Mrs. Langdon," I said to the housekeeper, which was certainly the truth. (Langdon was her second husband's last name, from whom she had divorced.)

We five trooped up the stairs, figured out which was the master bedroom and opened the door. There was Joanne, in bed. Alone.

"Well, we're all here, aren't we?" she said, not seeming terribly surprised.

"Yes, but where's the rest of us?" I asked, as coolly as I could, given my surprise at not finding Coleman in the room.

"Down the hall," she said, as if nothing out of the ordinary had just occurred.

All the while the "photographer" was snapping shots of her in bed. Finally she said, "That's enough pictures." We all then marched down the hall, opened another door, and there was Coleman, in bed. The photographer got busy again. When he was done with those pictures, they left the room.

"Well, now you've got what you want," I said to Coleman. "You are going to be single again."

"You're what I want," he said and then added, "I knew you would come."

I knew Jackson didn't tell him, but perhaps calling at a late hour and not finding me at home gave him a clue. I didn't know, and I most definitely didn't care.

Our business finished (and with no breaking in necessary!), the PIs and I went to a roadside diner for breakfast. We sat in a big booth with one of those individual jukeboxes. I put in money and played a few songs. My "associates" were dumbfounded. They said in previous situations like this, the women were basket cases, but I seemed euphoric. Which is exactly how I felt.

I called my mother after breakfast and told her things went really well—except they were not in bed together. That would have been nice. (I never did understand exactly why. Who has an affair but doesn't share a bed, anyway?) Nonetheless, he was

in her house. Mother asked how I was. I told her I was terrific. She said she'd probably never understand me, in that little
things could throw me for a loop but I could sail right through
the big things. I really was happy as a lark for the first time in
many years.

Our gang drove to Logan Airport and flew to Chicago. When
I got home, guess who was standing in the foyer? Indeed, the man
of the hour.

"What took you so long?" he asked.

Well, I told him, we had to get to Boston and get on a plane.

"You should have come with me," he said. "I chartered one."

Then the lawyer meetings started. He said he was going to sue
my analyst for alienation of affection. (I am not kidding.) His
resistance to a divorce was not because ours was the love story of
the century; it's that he wanted to keep things as they were. The
children and I were like props in his play. And of course he did
not wish to lose my parents as in-laws.

We finally hammered out a divorce agreement, and I went
along with joint custody because his interest in the children was
so minimal that agreeing to any kind of shared custody was mean-
ingless. The settlement was not exactly what I (or anyone else)
would call equitable, but nothing would change about the way
I lived, and ultimately I was pleased. Furthermore, he would
pay the children's bills off into the sunset. He asked for all the
valuable art, no doubt expecting a fight. I said fine. The way
I looked at it was that he had selected it, it was his money that
paid for it and, to be honest, I thought it was an effective way to
make the statement that it was worth anything to get rid of him.

It was definitely a "fuck you" message, whether he understood it that way or not.

Once everything was worked out, Coleman begged me for another chance. He essentially said, "I can do better. We can be a family. I'm going to get a weekend house, and you have to give me a chance, if only for the children." There was a legal mechanism by which I could keep the settlement we had agreed to in place while co-habiting, so I thought what the hell? Let's see what he can do, though I was beyond skeptical at that point.

My idea of a weekend house was a little A-frame in the woods. Coleman's was the Swift estate in Lake Forest, across from the Bath & Tennis Club on Green Bay Road (where he certainly would not have been welcome, as it was restricted). The house was what Abra, then almost eight years old, called "an English two-door mansion." It was on ten acres of land with a pool, tennis court, and greenhouse. And he bought it furnished, so at the beginning of the summer we moved our act to Lake Forest: Coleman, me, the kids and the domestic staff. Of course, nothing changed except the scenery. He was still absent, still chilly, and I had my answer. We went back to the city earlier than I'd planned because I had a scare one night (with no Mr. Coleman in residence) when I heard a voice somewhere on the grounds.

"Heeeelp me! Heeeelp me!" it sounded like someone was screaming.

I called the police department and identified myself, telling them that someone was being assaulted on my property.

They said they'd be right over, so I went to my second-floor bedroom window, where I was easily spotted, wearing a white nightgown. I saw them drive onto the property and they saw me in the window. After about ten minutes they returned to the house, and like Cyrano delivering his message to Roxanne, one of the officers said to the lady in the window: "There is no one on the property, Mrs. Coleman. Two of the neighbor's peacocks got loose, and that's the noise they make."

The next day we packed up and I knew once and for all I was a city girl. And soon to be a single one, at that. I did have a moment of concern for the gardener, however. Three of the four families who had lived in that house had divorced, so the poor guy never knew who he would be working for.

Though I may not have been aware of what I was doing, I had put myself through the test of deciding when enough is enough. Over the years countless readers wrote to me, asking, in essence, "How do you know when things are unfixable, and how do you know when enough *is* enough?" All marriages, certainly, involve putting up with things you wish were different, making allowances and figuring out where irritants fit on the importance scale. Sometimes a rocky marriage can be repaired, and sometimes it can't. I think a person knows when it's not worth trying anymore if, in the dark of night, they just know that anything would be better than what's going on. Making that determination is not unlike the Supreme Court decision regarding pornography: you may not be able to define it, but you know it when you see it.

Age also figured into the equation for me. When I called it a day with Coleman, I was twenty-eight years old, with far more of my life in front of me than behind me. I have advised older women in precarious financial circumstances to remain legally married but to make themselves scarce. Individual values figure in, as well. Some people just want to be married, no matter the baggage. Others must consider money. And the truth is that people have varying thresholds of pain and tolerance. In any event, the tests I put myself through during the course of our marriage were: trying to live my own life while ignoring him; considering lifestyle poultices (i.e., an affair, a job); and deciding, with a therapist's help, that I could, and would, make a life on my own, if necessary. I had not one doubt that divorce was what needed to happen next.

When we separated I was in the enviable position of not having people wonder what went wrong or whose "fault" it was. Everyone understood why I unloaded him. The children seemed unsurprised by it. The younger two didn't even know their father very well, and Abra, when I told her, said, "You know, Mom, he doesn't tell the truth." Some years later, all three of them said that they never could see their father and me together. I do think that Abra felt the backlash of the divorce in ways the younger two did not, and this did indeed manifest later. I know from my work, and from friends, that there is often one kid who suffers from a divorce more than the others, and often it's the eldest. It frankly never occurred to me to keep it together "for the children." I am convinced that a tension-free home with one parent is preferable to a situation where there is fighting or frost, and I always advised such to anyone who wrote to me asking for my opinion on this matter.

Alas, he did not go quietly. Instead, he checked into the Menninger Clinic in Topeka, Kansas (a fancy psychiatric hospital where my mother was on the board!) and embarked on eighteen months of therapy. That is a pretty long time to try to deal with your "issues." My guess is that he believed I would not go ahead and divorce a guy who was in the bin.

He guessed wrong. Not only did I continue with the legalities, but I also would not go visit him, as he requested. I simply could not have a guy in an institution begging me to give him one more chance. I did, however, send the children, with Jackson, to visit him. One day his social worker called to say she understood I was not coming down. That was true, I told her, though I did not wish to impede his treatment and would gladly talk to her on the phone about anything she wished. (I never thought he went with a pure heart, and my father said he parked himself there to sit out a bad money market.) In any case, during my first—and only—talk with the social worker, I asked if he had mentioned his alcohol problem. "His *what*?" As I said, I did not think he went there with a pure heart.

When he did choose to return to Chicago, he took an apartment on Lake Shore Drive. After a two-year separation, we were finally divorced, and Coleman married Joanne Field Pirovano Langdon shortly thereafter. That marriage lasted a grand total of thirty days and then was annulled for reasons unknown to me.

Later, about fifteen years after we'd been legally divorced, he was richer than ever. He was, in fact, one place off the Forbes 400 list, sort of like a runner-up. But as he continued to get richer, he also continued to spend more money paying lawyers. His litigiousness really heated up, and he seemed to thrive on suing or being sued. There was even a story written about his serial engagement of dozens of law firms in *American Lawyer*. He became notorious for not paying his bills, which was the reason he had to deal with so many law firms.

Coleman went on to make some high-profile hotel investments—notably buying the Navarro in New York City and the Fairfax in Washington, D.C., to make them Ritz Carltons. He was a pioneer in boutique hotels, starting with buying the Whitehall Hotel Chicago, and then buying the Chestnut Towers, which he renamed The Tremont (after a famous street in downtown Boston). Whether it was because he wore out his welcome or because bigger ponds beckoned, he moved to Washington. Then he moved to New York, remarried a fourth time, and had two more children. He later divorced his fourth wife and lived through a widely publicized bankruptcy, from which he recovered, to a degree. For perhaps multiple reasons, his fortune diminished, the art was sold, and he went from living in a grand apartment on E. 72nd Street to living in hotels. The kids said his spending was driven by manic episodes and his reputation was such that "doing deals" was no longer in the cards.

Over the years (even now, 44 years later!) people who either knew him or his reputation have asked how I could have been married to him. I have never had a good answer to the question. With all the pushback about my decision to marry him—and my rejection of it—I was, in retrospect, exercising my prerogative to make my own decisions. I was flying in the face of good judgment because I'd gotten it into my head that I was right and "they" were wrong. Like Icarus, I displayed hubris. I had simply made up my mind, and with the recklessness of the young I could not imagine getting burned.

My determination to prove everyone wrong was certainly a denial of the obvious. And with this particular man there was the aspect of tying my wagon to someone who was "different." God knows I had never met anyone like him. I was being the adventuress with zero thought of any consequences, or any consideration that all the people who told me not to go through with it might be right. Trying to make sense of that disastrous marriage from the vantage point of time, analysis, and, I hope, wisdom, it is clear to me that I saw Coleman as a challenge, whether I acknowledged it or not. He was a reclamation project, for sure. At an unconscious level, I must have found him dangerous (which he proved to be, for my mental health) but at the same time mysteriously exciting and smart. The "good" prototype for this was my father, who was successful, smart, and exciting, but what my father was—and Coleman wasn't—was a charismatic, warm person who was a loving father. Clearly I was coloring outside the lines with Coleman in a deluded "I know best" mindset. Such difficult, unreachable men come with a price tag, and often a fatal flaw.

Bucking my parents—particularly my mother—was an aberrational anomaly in my life. With hindsight, I believe it to have been a misguided attempt at independence and autonomy. How I wish I had acted out by, say, remaining single until I was thirty.

CHAPTER THREE

*Wherein I am sort of single—
no decree yet—and stumble into
the news business.*

Emotionally, if not legally, I was single—and feeling elated. I knew this was unusual, but hell, much of my life was half a beat off. With Coleman "away" at Menninger's, a friend of his was acting as conservator, and I had a generous monthly allowance. I think my frame of mind at the time can best be summed up by one spur of the moment, malevolent and joyful act: I gave away Coleman's $15,000 Hasselblad to one of our elevator men— a symbolic (if misguided) expression of the fact that I regarded Coleman as permanently gone, along with his fancy camera. It frankly never occurred to me to sell it because money was not the problem.

For many years, about many subjects, I have said jokingly, "The Lord will provide." Sure enough, as word of my changed status and new circumstances got around town, one of the great gifts of my life soon presented itself to me. It all started with my first social invitation after the divorce was initiated. It could not have been more perfect: it was to a wedding in a family I'd known since I was a teenager. Sheldon Gray and I had dated and I'd gotten to know his whole family. And what an interesting family they were. Mae and Joe Gray, Sheldon's parents, had a sister and brother-in-law who had died within five years of each other, leaving three young children. These youngsters were absorbed into the Gray household, which already consisted of three children, and although they were cousins, the six children referred to themselves as brothers and sisters. The cousins who were raised as siblings to the Gray children were the Siskels. Visiting the Grays in Glencoe, I had met Genie Siskel, "the baby," when he was nine!

Mae Gray, knowing that I was newly separated, thoughtfully and decorously decided that Genie would be my dinner partner at the wedding. No one would mistake him for a date because he was obviously younger than I, and I would not have to be on my own. Then in his early twenties, he was the surprisingly young film critic for the *Chicago Tribune*. It turned out that, thanks to the thoughtfulness of Mae Gray, I got a life-changing gift: a career, and the astonishing realization that I could write.

I must have talked Genie's ear off during dinner, because at evening's end he said it seemed as though I knew everyone and I was very funny.

"Can you write?" he asked me.

"I don't know," I answered, which was the odd but honest truth. A little peculiar, in retrospect, that I didn't just say no.

He then asked if I would talk to his editor at the *Tribune* if he could get him to see me, and I agreed. To my surprise, the aforementioned gentleman, the features editor of the *Tribune*, asked to see me at two o'clock the following Friday.

Genie gave me a little background on the gentleman prior to the meeting. Walter Simmons had been a foreign correspondent who had been tapped to be the features editor. He was in his sixties, gruff, and he generally terrified people—though Genie was a favorite of his.

At the appointed hour I bounced into Simmons's office. He indeed seemed foreboding and dour. Tall and portly, he had red cheeks and white hair. Imagine a dyspeptic Santa Claus. He spoke in a low, slow monotone.

"Siskel probably doesn't know his ass from his elbow about spotting writers, but what the hell?" This was the greeting.

Then he asked what I had written that he could see.

I gave him an unfiltered answer that was guaranteed to do me no good.

"Uh, nothing. Well, no. Wait. I did write one long piece about being a Playboy Bunny."

He said he'd like to see it and asked me to come back with it the following week.

I brought him my typescript of the piece, along with the photograph of me wearing rabbit ears, high heels, and, basically, a corset. He read it as I sat there.

"I'm going to run this, and you will work for me," he said.

I was truly floored. After a few days he sent me his edits to my draft—to which I paid close attention—and the week after that he ran the piece in the paper's Sunday features section. On the cover. With the picture. A three-thousand-word cover story was my introduction to the public and the newspaper business. That nice man had decided to make me a star, and he did.

My style was conversational, to say the least, and I have since learned that to write as one speaks is uncommon. My mother and I shared this talent—if that's what it is. Often, a wonderful journalist is a so-so conversationalist, or an engaging raconteur can't write. Both Mother and I were often told, "Reading you is like hearing you talk." It is probably no accident that neither of us had any journalism training. Or as Simmons said when I mentioned that fact, "Good. No bullshit to unlearn."

What I did instinctively well was skewer sacred cows. It was finally useful that I was a critical observer by nature. I suspect that I was snarky when snarky wasn't cool. Simmons's instructions were to pick a subject and write two to three thousand words about it. These were always Sunday cover pieces, and they took me three to four weeks to write. There was minimal research involved, sometimes only a trip (for example, to Palm Beach to make fun of the wealthy excess of Worth Avenue). And then I would basically write an essay—always funny and opinionated, and sometimes destructive. I had zero reporting chops, so I was writing from my head. One early piece created a buzz because of a phrase I had coined: "Dancing for Disease." I wondered why there were all these fancy parties for sicknesses (a Cancer Ball, a Diabetes Gala, etc.). Why couldn't people just write a check and stay home? After talking to a few party planners and physicians, I'd learned that some diseases were "sexy." Others were not. Heart disease and cancer, for example, were considered sexy. Epilepsy, sadly, not so much.

I was thrilled that Simmons was a fan of my work, though I undoubtedly owed some of his goodwill to Mrs. Simmons. She was a former newswoman herself and apparently liked my pieces, which he would relay to me. Before long, I was calling him Papa Bear.

It is always perilous to start at the top, and I knew there was a collective eye roll going on at all four Chicago papers about this babe with Gloria Steinem hair and a Rolls Royce waltzing into the *Tribune* to write Sunday cover pieces. My "discovery" was viewed as Brenda Starr as told to Cinderella.

People in the newsroom could not believe my success, and people *outside* the paper could not believe I was even there! Real newspaper people worked years for such a break, and I was aware of that. In the beginning I had only one supportive well-wisher (besides Siskel and Simmons). Dorothy Storck was a senior reporter who was a former foreign correspondent and then a columnist. She reached out the hand of friendship and told me my stuff was witty and different, and to ignore the people whose noses were out of joint. I was, of course, happy to have a few people in my corner, but I had a deep understanding that the news business, in which I had essentially grown up, cannot support no-talent nepotism. The work product is too public. It is out there in the world, and if your work is mediocre, they have to get rid of you. I knew people were saying I'd slept with someone in the composing room, or my mother had "bought it for me" (even though she was at the *Chicago Sun-Times*, a rival paper), but I knew in time those opinions would change. And they did.

After about six months of my irregularly timed, lengthy features, Papa Bear called me in and said an odd thing was happening: people were phoning the *Tribune*, asking to see more pieces by me on a regular basis. He said the next logical step was a column.

"Do you think you can do that?"

"No," I said, definitively.

He countered that he was sure I could, with his guidance.

"How about three a week?"

"*Absolutely* not," I said, explaining I'd never had a job—of any kind—and could not imagine churning out regular newspaper columns.

"Well then, two," he said.

I demurred. Papa Bear assured me I could handle that and promised to whip me into shape.

"I've been around a long time," he said, "and I know you can do this."

Sure thing, I thought, *if God drops everything else.*

Oddly enough, because columns had to come in at just 750 words, I discovered it was very comfortable for me to write short. I had a knack for getting in and getting out. The column was called, simply, "Margo." You know, like Hildegard or Liberace. I was free to choose my own topics (not being trained to specialize in a particular field) and so my subjects became a mélange of opinion essays, reports of events, riffs on publishing, politics, the theater—and sometimes lunch interviews. All the public relations offices in Chicago were offering me people or events for the column.

There is no way to say this modestly, so I'll just say it: very soon out of the gate, mine was considered *the* fun interview in Chicago, probably because my questions were not the obvious ones, and as a columnist I had the leeway to be funny and state opinions; a reporter did not.

There was something else about my column that was unusual: my stuff went straight to the *Tribune* lawyers to be vetted. Dr. David Reuben, for example, author of *Everything You Always Wanted to Know About Sex (But Were Afraid to Ask)*, threatened to sue me if I wrote about him again. All I had said was that his Q & A format read like a cross between Helen Gurley Brown and *Popular Mechanics*, that I found his to be a cutesy-Kinsey approach, and that his competitiveness with other authors regarding sales struck me as unseemly.

Papa Bear said, relative to me and the legal department, "You are the star in my crown and the thorn in my side."

Another column I wrote led to a change in the rules at the paper. It was only after I interviewed "Louisiana Fats" (Chicago's Cardinal John Cody, my old neighbor) that all *Tribune* interviewers had to start using a tape recorder, in addition to taking notes, because His Eminence said he didn't say something that I said he said. (He said it.)

It turned out writing was easy and I found it a lot of fun. I became known for my ledes—journalism's purposely misspelled word for "lead," the opening sentence of any story. Lunching with Zsa Zsa Gabor in The Pump Room, she spied an ex-lover across the room and handed me the lede when she said, "Husbands are so possessive, dollink, they always vant to know who you're dating." Hearing A&P grocery heir Huntington Hartford tell me of his financial flops—for example, a coating for statues that repelled pigeon poop—it took hardly any time at all for me to come up with, "They say money talks. It sometimes says goodbye."

After six months as a *Tribune* columnist there were offers from different newspaper syndicates. This I could barely believe. I just assumed I would go with the Chicago Tribune-New York News Syndicate because I was a *Tribune* property. The hitch, however, was that it was Dear Abby's syndicate, my dear aunt Popo, with whom I'd never gotten along, and she told them she would be "displeased" if they took me. John McMeel, then brand new in the business, wanted me, but Papa Bear said his group was too green. Actually, the top syndicate at the time was my mother's, the Field Newspaper Syndicate, but I feared that *would* look like nepotism—plus it would require my moving to the *Chicago Daily*

News. I did not want to be disloyal to Papa Bear and leave. He, however, told me he was a year away from retirement.

"The name of the game in this business is syndication, and I want you to go," he said, and gave me his blessing.

I asked Mother if it would be all right with her. She said, "Come on over!" and sent me an IBM Selectric — just like hers — as a welcome gift. I got off to a fast start and had a wonderful roster of client papers. I was in most major cities in the country — still writing as "Margo." Syndicated features then required three pieces a week, but having become accustomed to doing two, I stretched and managed.

Freedom, strangely enough, became my biggest problem. I had no field. I could write about anything. (My nonfield was called "social commentary.") At least Siskel and Ebert knew what they were supposed to write about. I really had to hustle. There were times when I was writing about things from my own life. One column was based on Jackson's report about the hierarchy at the playground. I named it "The Nanny Mafia." Then Tom Wolfe's lawyers got in touch with the lawyers at the *Tribune* to say that was *his* phrase. When the Kirkland & Ellis lawyer handling my column asked me for some background, I said that I would take on the (then) single and childless Mr. Wolfe any ol' day regarding the workings of the nanny mafia. Of course nothing happened. I actually met him some years later, in 1977, and relayed the story. He laughed and said the complaint did not come from him and that his lawyers were "protective."

With time, I learned the syndicate business was quite political. When my home paper, the *Chicago Daily News,* dropped "Dear Beth," the advice column for teenagers based at the *Boston Globe,* the *Globe* dropped me. The *St. Louis Post-Dispatch* canceled me when I made fun of the Veiled Prophet Ball—the pet charity of the publisher's wife. My favorite cancelation was worth it—just to tell the story. It was the *Cleveland Plain Dealer*. I'd read a wire service story about a sequestered jury where the wife of a locked-up juror told a reporter she was sure there was hanky-panky going on with the jurors in the hotel. I should mention that Daryle Feldmeir, my editor at the *Daily News*, also the editor-in-chief, was as wonderful to me as Papa Bear had been. He was also an envelope-pusher who allowed me to use double entendres, so I wrote a riff on the disgruntled wife of the sequestered juror, and ended the piece by saying, "I guess this gives new meaning to the term 'hung jury.'" Well, the wife of the publisher told her husband that I was too dirty for her taste, and I was removed from the *Plain Dealer*.

I really was having a wonderful time doing this thing my parents had never talked to me about: working. And the biggest surprise of all was that I was making substantial money.

Having a career is the thing that put me on the path to finally becoming an independent adult. It is not a substitute for a fulfilling personal life, certainly, but if it's work that engages you, the reward is a different kind of happiness. It is validation, and something that can add purpose to a life. Having to work is not usually a choice, so I always advised people that if their job wasn't great or didn't offer satisfaction—if it was merely a paycheck—they should volunteer somewhere in their spare time, to tamp down heartbreak or loss by feeling useful. Doing something for someone else can be tonic when your own life feels like it's gone off the rails. I first heard this idea from my mother. When things aren't going well, work that engages you is a great place to hide. For me, going to work in a field I had coincidentally grown up in gave me purpose, identity and my own place in the community. Had I stayed married, I doubt that working would have ever entered the picture. For me, one door closed and another one opened, wide and welcoming.

CHAPTER FOUR

Wherein lovely men doing interesting things fill my social calendar while a two-year separation finally becomes a divorce.

"The mist of time," as John Huston referred to memories, has the power to leave in its wake more impressions than specifics, more feelings than facts. While I know there were downtimes, the only real angst I remember was the fear that the legalities of the divorce would drag on forever. The two years it took before the divorce was final seemed like four, and as any divorced person will tell you, there is palpable relief in finally and formally being disentangled from a spouse who in every other way is gone from your life, or as "gone" as someone can be who is the other parent of your young children. But the liberation I felt at having made the decision, along with getting the hang of living as an independent adult, more than compensated for whatever anxiety I felt while waiting for the divorce to be finalized.

I am well aware that my situation was different from that of many others'. Money was not a concern, I was living in my hometown where I had already been established, pre-husband, and I had the moral support of my parents. I also had a great job. During this time I had some comfortable romances which served to remind me of the BC (Before Coleman) years when men were caring companions, not adversaries and bringers of distress. Moreover, friends were extraordinarily kind. During the first summer of my separation from Coleman, Marty and Anne

Peretz invited me, the kids and Jackson to spend the summer with them on Cape Cod — and they even found a house for me to rent that was near them in Wellfleet. As I was by then a newly fledged columnist who had deadlines, the Cape was creative manna from heaven for a city girl like me who regarded the outdoors as a place where the birds flew around uncooked. I wrote about things like Anne and me getting arrested by the "shellfish constable" (his official title) because we were clamming without a license. I wrote about getting lost in my own winding, sandy driveway and having to tie strips of white rags to the trees — a Chicago girl's adaptation of Gretel's breadcrumbs.

I was present, courtesy of the Peretzes, at the founding of "The Academy of the Overrated." The host was the literary and social critic Irving Howe, and present were painter Robert Motherwell, political scientist Richard Neustadt, and sociologist Nat Glazer. This group decided who deserved their eminent reputations and who did not. I, of course, wrote about this extremely highbrow, intellectual dish — naming names — creating national laughter and, I suppose, some hard feelings. Buckminster Fuller cannot have been pleased to have been named the architect for the Academy's clubhouse. Ditto Norman Cousins, who had such enthusiastic backing he was made chairman of the board. Motherwell nominated Andrew Wyeth for membership into the Academy (he received unanimous approval). People like Andy Warhol, Margaret Mead, C. P. Snow, Gian Carlo Menotti and Arthur Miller fairly sailed in. Arthur Goldberg secured the job of in-house counsel, and Marshall McLuhan was voted secretary of communications. Archibald MacLeish ("Archie" to them) was made poet laureate. Gore Vidal's name came up, but he was blackballed. "No one ever overrates Gore," the players agreed.

Coretta Scott King was awarded *two* seats, both as a woman and a black. Thank heaven this slaughter of sacred cows was not without moments of respect and mercy. Norman Mailer, Saul Bellow, George Balanchine and Picasso formed the small but prestigious group whose talents were considered quite as substantial as the public thought they were. Mike McGrady at *Newsday* so loved this column that he asked if he could run it, giving me credit. This was quite a compliment for a greenhorn. I was beginning to feel I had found my place in the world, and it was in print.

I was deeply grateful to the Peretzes for their loving friendship. They included me in everything they did that summer and took me everywhere, which is how I wound up at Dr. Robert Jay Lifton's party marking the anniversary of Hiroshima. An expert on war and violence, Lifton's party remembering the bombing and burning was an annual event. Having an eye for the smaller details, I couldn't help notice that Mrs. Lifton served barbequed chicken wings…an unusual choice, I thought, given that particular occasion. Another memorable party was at Bernard Malamud's house. He was funny and flattering. For whatever reason, he glued himself to my side for about fifteen minutes, and his coda to our conversation was an invitation to dinner for when I came to New York. "But only for dinner!" he stipulated. I don't know how he decided I was Alma Mahler dying to strike up a romance, but I thought he was adorable.

The Lord certainly was providing. The timing of my flight from Mr. Right #1 was definitely auspicious for a girl who had stumbled into a newspaper career. The last years of the 1960s coincided with a turbulent and chaotic time in American politics. Both Dr. Martin Luther King, Jr. and Robert Kennedy were assassinated. The infamous 1968 Democratic National Convention in

Chicago (at which my old boss, Hubert Humphrey, was nominated) saw riots in the park with police beating civilians—most of them young people who had come to protest racism, American policies and the Vietnam War. One of the better organized groups in town—and in the park—was the Youth International Party, better known as the Yippies, led by Abbie Hoffman and Jerry Rubin. I was camped out at the Hilton with the Gene McCarthy camp, at the invitation of Marty Peretz. The Hilton was across from the park, and we spent time in the lobby helping people who staggered in, many of them bloody. The Yippies would go on trial in 1969 to 1970 as the "Conspiracy Seven." The Chinese curse had come to pass: may you live in interesting times. Though the country was in spasms, it was an exciting time to be in the news business.

If Walter Simmons and Daryle Feldmeir were my mentors, J. Anthony Lukas was my journalism school. Previously a foreign correspondent, he was then the *New York Times* bureau chief in Chicago, and their offices were in the Tribune Tower. Mutual friends said we should meet, but we actually met on our own in the hall. He stopped me to ask some innocuous question, and we introduced ourselves and started to talk. He mentioned that he had won "The Prize." I knew he meant the Pulitzer but could not resist asking if it was cold in Sweden, simply because he had called it "The Prize," generally understood to be the Nobel. (He would later go on to win a second Pulitzer.) We became an item, as they say, and I called him my Jewish raccoon because of the discernible dark circles under his eyes—from pigmentation, not fatigue.

My relationship with him is worth recalling not just because his was a famous name in journalism, but also because the times

in which we found ourselves were so attention-grabbing in terms
of the country's politics, and we were immersed in the events of
the time. What was going on then is not all that unconnected
from the unrest and division we are living through now. Although
he was a serious journalist and author (he wrote *The Barnyard
Epithet and Other Obscenities: Notes on the Chicago Conspiracy
Trial* while we were together) he was extremely generous about
reading my mostly humorous essays, making suggestions, and
answering technical questions. It was serendipity that I would have
a beau who was at the upper tier of my new career. I learned years
later that he was a real hero to younger journalists. And we went
through the remarkable Conspiracy Seven trial together—he the
old pro, I the novice. Not to anyone's credit, it became our social
life. The journalists and the defendants (plus William Kunstler,
the lead defense attorney) often partied together in the evenings.
I suspect such a thing would not happen today.

The Conspiracy Seven had an office, barely furnished, in
a dumpy downtown building. Lukas and I went there one day
after court, soon after the trial had begun. When we walked in,
Abbie Hoffman was standing on a table giving a pep talk to his
fellow defendants, lawyers, and random hangers-on. Abbie and
I had been at Brandeis together—he was a senior when I was
a freshman. Looking back, it was hard to believe this was the same
well-mannered young man who drove a Corvette and wore tennis
whites. We had known each other to the extent that we would play
gin rummy (I would lose) and I would buy submarine sandwiches
from him when he came through our dorm. When he saw me with
Lukas (who was referred to as "the New York Times") he yelled,
"Margo! Let's fuck!" I was mortified, and doubly so because this
had not been an activity in which we had ever engaged.

Party central was the home of Jim Hoge and his then-wife, Alice (now Arlen). Hoge was, at the time, editor of the *Sun-Times*. In town from New York were Jason Epstein, the fabled Random House editor, and William Styron. They annexed themselves to our merry band. Because the Federal Building, where the trial was taking place, was diagonally across from the Standard Club, Epstein asked if he could stay there on my membership. It would certainly be convenient to be housed across the street. I said yes, but I would need very precise documentation from Random House, explaining that my estranged husband was "away" and I didn't want there to be any question of my keeping a gentleman friend at his downtown club.

In fact, it was in the Standard Club dining room that Lukas and I made some mischief. All the federal judges were members, offering the club prestige and the judges proximity. The Conspiracy Seven trial judge, called "Little Judge Hoffman" (he really was a tiny person), lunched there every day. We decided to ruin his lunch—which we did—by inviting Abbie Hoffman (no relation) to lunch with us. The little judge was apoplectic and of course had no idea how the scruffy defendant had gotten in there in the first place.

While the trial for me was a social event (I was not covering, obviously) it took a great toll on Tony and was the reason he left the *Times*. The desk in New York was altering his copy, not believing that what he was filing could actually be what was going on. I remember our seeing the Costa-Gavras movie *Z* and watching tears run down his cheek. He said that was where we were going, as a country. When the trial was over he left the paper, choosing to work for the *New York Times Sunday Magazine* as a way station. Then he left daily journalism to write books—perhaps his most famous was *Common Ground: A Turbulent Decade in the Lives of Three American Families*, the story of Boston's school desegregation as seen from the vantage point of three families.

An odd thing, considering he was truly a gifted journalist, was that he had really wanted to be an actor. His uncle was the movie star Paul Lukas, whom he asked to come see him when he performed in a theatrical at Harvard. Uncle Paul came and suggested he was not cut out for the stage or films and to perhaps look elsewhere for his life's work. At that point, he dedicated himself to the Harvard *Crimson*, where he would begin a lifelong frenemy relationship with David Halberstam. When he left Chicago and the *Times*, I urged him to go into therapy, which he ultimately did. He suffered from depression, which he believed took root after his mother's suicide when he was nine years old. He took my advice, but treatment, in the end, was not successful. We might have married but for the fact that he was terrified of the three young children who would come with my part of the deal; and, on my end, having tried to "fix" someone before, I knew such repairs were not within my power, and I wasn't going to make that mistake again. We remained dear friends, however.

At some point after he had left town he called me from, I think, Ohio, and asked if he could fly in for lunch, saying he needed to talk to me. We arranged it for the following day and met at the Cape Cod Room at the Drake Hotel. He was devastated because Nora Ephron (whom he had dated before me) wrote a story for *Esquire* about the literati in New York giving each other crabs. With the characters thinly disguised, she wrote an offhand sexual remark about Lukas because, I guess, as her mother famously told her, "Everything is copy." He was terribly wounded by such a personal thing winding up in print, and I did what I could to talk him down. We remained friends until, at age 64, he, like his mother, took his own life.

I want to mention one other man I went out with during this time of my life. We saw each other only three times, and while it never became romantic, the connection between him, *Love Story*, and my later life involved a twist of fate that, to this day, leaves people wide-eyed. For the connection you will have to wait until the last chapter, but the man was Erich Segal. We were fixed up by Genie Siskel, who had been Segal's student at Yale. Our first date was in Chicago. Segal was a great runner, and he wanted to take a run before our dinner. We met at his hotel, the Ambassador, just as he returned from running. He asked if I wanted to wait in his suite while he changed, and I said no, I was happy waiting in the lobby, and sat down to read. Then—and not for the first time—I was mistaken for a "working girl." A strange man walked over to me and said, "I don't suppose..." I cut him off and said his supposition was right, and went back to reading my magazine. I must say this time I was calmer about such an offer than I had been maybe four or five years earlier at the Beverly Hills Hotel. At that time I had been in the lobby when a man sidled up to me and said, "Would $10,000 convince you to come upstairs with me?" Far from being cool, I shrieked my incredulity—"WHAT?!"—and he quickly disappeared.

Erich returned to the lobby, dressed, and we went on to have a lovely, talky evening. I found him to be totally asexual but great fun to be with. He said he was catching hell for having written the screenplay for the Beatles' *Yellow Submarine* and *Love Story*. He was denied tenure at Yale because his theatrical diversions disturbed his department. His expertise on Plautus was not enough to save him. I didn't write a column about him until sometime later when I defended his going on the *Tonight Show* and comparing himself to Dostoevsky.

Some weeks after our first meeting he phoned me from New Haven.

"Do you want to go to the movies?" he asked.

"Sure," I said, figuring he was returning to Chicago and this was just a request for dinner and a movie.

"Meet me in New York," he said, giving me a date and time a few weeks hence.

The movie he was inviting me to, of course, was the premiere of *Love Story*. We were staying in different hotels, and he called me when I got in. Considering his accomplishments and education, he was surprisingly unsophisticated.

"What if we can't get a cab?" he said, sounding very worried.

"Erich," I told him, "You are the screenwriter. Tell the studio to send a car."

It was a very big-deal movie, and unusual, because the studio told him to write a book to come out before the movie, so everyone would know the story. At the theater we met Cynthia, his uber-Jewish mother. She was wearing a large campaign-style button that said: "I am Erich Segal's mother." That movie, of course, had a phrase that permanently entered the lexicon: "Love means never having to say you're sorry." It was a gala night and a big hit, notwithstanding critic Judith Crist calling it "Camille with bullshit."

CHAPTER FIVE

Wherein I again make a bum choice, only this time it is well thought out.

I take heart from the saying, "Every woman should have a forgettable second husband."

There. Now I have just ruined the suspense.

After having a couple of euphoric years as a gay divorcée, I decided it was time to stop entertaining myself and get back to being married. Somehow I made the decision that the time had come for me to focus on selecting Mr. Right #2. It honestly never occurred to me to continue what I was doing—which was being on my own and having quite a super social life. I wanted a second chance, a second husband and, most of all, a functional father for my children. I had already been swept off my feet once, and not exactly by Fred Astaire.

This time the selection process was decidedly more thoughtful because I knew what I was looking for—or at least what I thought was required: a middle-class guy who did not live for his business, was not a social mountaineer, had no weirdness to speak of and wanted to be a family man. It almost goes without saying that he had to be a moderate drinker or a nondrinker altogether. (I did actually consider scoping out Alcoholics Anonymous meetings until a friend said, with no stab at delicacy at all, "Are you nuts?") The next husband had to be for the kids; a surrogate father and a "normal" partner—assuming I would know "normal" when

I saw it. Finding a suitable husband and father moved to the top of my to-do list.

I landed on a man named Jules Furth, whom I had occasionally seen over the years at different social functions in Chicago. We knew of each other, but we didn't actually know each other. The first time we really talked was at a party at The Standard Club. Much of the conversation we had that first time was about a "situation" from which I needed to extricate myself. This was before the word *stalker* had any currency, but in spirit, that's what it was—even if by letter from London. I had met a wicked handsome British newscaster for Independent Television News (ITN) at the Pugwash Conference for Science and World Affairs held at the University of Chicago (where I had been a local "hostess") and we embarked on a truly short romance. It was short because he wore silk briefs with no fly in the front; told me he could send coded messages from the combination lock on his briefcase, and said he was an operative for MI-something... 5 or 6. Mercifully, he had to return to work in England. I had told him I didn't think we should stay in touch, but was inundated with letters from him nonetheless. I had a good chum over there who was well connected, so I asked him if he'd ever heard of this person. My friend reported that the man was, in fact, an ITN newscaster—and a fortune hunter. (No mention of his being nuts, though.)

It was this messy situation about which I was whining to Jules Furth at The Standard Club. He was more than willing to be a shoulder to lean on, and he instructed me to write a hard-nosed letter saying I did not wish to be in touch anymore. Ever. He jokingly offered to act as my bodyguard should Mr. ITN wander back to Chicago. He asked me out for dinner, and by then I was thinking of him as a problem-solver. He was supportive and low-key, and he wasn't a lot of work.

Furth was built like a football player. He resembled Tom Jones—a man who never really appealed to me, but, as I said before, looks were never what did it for me. He was a real jock, which was something totally foreign to me: a scratch golfer and a referee for pee-wee hockey games. His great enthusiasm was professional hockey.

I had no knowledge of either of his passions. In fact, the first Blackhawks game he took me to was like nothing I had ever seen before. I watched for a while (an inning? a quarter?) and then said, "My God, they're on skates!" I found the game to be totally uninteresting, and violent in the bargain. There were players smashing into the heavy plastic wall that separated them from the spectators, and people were hollering and drinking. I gave the Blackhawks one more try after that—only this time I brought the Sunday papers with me. Furth's seats were a few rows down from those of Arthur Wirtz—the owner of the team. After about ten minutes of the stick-wielding roughnecks whizzing around the ice, an usher appeared and said to Furth: "Mr. Wirtz would like your guest to put the newspapers away." I knew who Wirtz was, so of course I put the papers back into the tote bag whence they came.

Furth was a rather intellectual choice on my part, which is not to say that he was an intellectual. He was not the reader I was, nor did politics or theater particularly interest him. What he lived for was sports. He did like the newspaper business, however, and I'm quite sure he preferred my work to his. He once suggested that he join me in writing my column, but I declined. It was not in the cards for us to be Evans and Novak.

Granted, there was chemical frisson. I was not operating entirely like an employment agency. And once again, my parents were not thrilled when I told them this was Mr. Right #2, but this time there were no bribes, or tears. They just felt he was rather ordinary. Father called him "The Puck," and Mother asked if I'd searched the world for a man with my father's first name. This wasn't the rush job that my broken engagement and first marriage had been, but neither was this a courtship that stretched out long enough for me to learn some of the things I realized—after the fact—that I should have known. I just *assumed* he would be good with the children, and it frankly never occurred to me that he might not be able to keep up with me in the brains department. I did love him, but when I look back, I realize I loved everyone I married...at the time.

There wasn't an elaborate or memorable proposal. Rather, we simply came to a gradual understanding that we would marry and drifted toward setting the date. His "regular guy" personality was soothing, and he was easygoing. I didn't have to question his honesty, and he was lovingly solicitous of me. Jules was "old Chicago," which even I was not. He was established and, I felt, comfortable in his skin. We didn't argue and the relationship was comfortable.

He gave me a big rock that had been in his family for generations...and what jazzy generations they had been. His maternal grandfather, a major player in the business of corrugated boxes, dated Sophie Tucker, the famous singer and comedienne who was "the last of the red-hot mamas" during the first half of the twentieth century. She was an entertainer known for her humor and risqué songs, and clearly was Bette Midler's inspiration. Bette often made reference to her in her act and named her only child Sophie. I liked Jules' mother, Carolyn, enormously. She had red hair, four husbands, and great legs. (I would eventually go on to have the first two, but alas, the third was never a possibility.)

Our marriage took place in a rabbi's study with my parents, his mother, two other couples, my three children and his only child, a son who was Adam's age. Afterwards there was a dinner at my parents' apartment. According to Wikipedia this was in 1972. I have never been good with dates.

I wore a diaphanous knee-length white, gold and red Dior dress. (This dress was so gorgeous I had a dressmaker redo it. Today it is a blouse.) The choice of *which* rabbi's study was a bit of a thorny issue due to the fact that the groom was a German-Jewish funeral director who belonged to five Temples (*five!*) because that's where the potential clients were. When they became *actual* clients, he never touched them—though he did have the requisite license. What he did was deal with the families and sell them things.

The funeral business is an awful one, and everyone I knew who was in it hated it. It is lucrative, however—or at least it was back then, before Jessica Mitford's book *The American Way of Death* gained traction. She savaged the industry, highlighting bizarre practices and products, one such being the "Fit-a-Fut Oxford, specially designed footwear for the discerning corpse." (Well, that's what the ad said.) Mitford opened the door for cremation to catch on, followed by "green societies" who wanted to put the deceased directly into the ground dressed in only a sheet. For those of you who have heard about satin-lined bronze caskets starting at $25,000, I'm sure you can see the problems caused for the funeral industry by Ms. Mitford and her disciples.

Furth never intended to go into that line of work, but it was his family's business, and during his junior year of college

his father had a coronary and he had to go home to pitch in.
He was never able to get out. The money, I learned, was in the
boxes. And the pitch was: "Mother" or "Father" (this is the way
he always referred to the deceased when talking to the children)
lived a first-class life, and therefore the send-off should be no less
luxurious. Translation: nothing less than a mahogany or bronze
casket would do. Another trick of the trade was that many of the
clients shuffled off this mortal coil in Florida; therefore, when
the (Chicago) children called to make arrangements, Furth
made a *very* strong pitch to them to instruct the corresponding
funeral home handling the body to put it on the plane in the
very simplest, no frills, preferably pine box so that the "real"
final resting place could be purchased from him — in the city
"Mother" or "Father" had called home.

Another part of this odd occupation was that it was considered an "honor" if the funeral director and his wife would pay
a shiva call. Once we were married, I acquiesced because this was
my husband, and this is what he did. I had always been willing
to function as "Mrs. Financier" during my previous marriage, so
now I was "Mrs. Funeral Director" in this one. I once said to my
mother about these social calls, "I wish that I could shiva like
my sister Kate."

Back then, when you traveled and checked into a hotel, the
registration form asked for your occupation. Furth always wrote,
"sports writer." (As I said, his was a business no one was really
thrilled about.) And he did, in fact, write some sports articles for
a suburban paper. Something else peculiar to this industry came
in a piece of advice Furth's father had given him: never visit
a friend in the hospital who is really sick. It would be too sug-
gestive, if not bad luck. The Yiddish word for what this would

make you is "Malakh-Amoves," the angel of death. In other words, a funeral director's presence would not be taken well and might, in fact, be confused with being a bid for business.

Our honeymoon was my first experience with sailing. He chartered a yacht with a crew of five which left from Piraeus and visited various Greek Islands. We would pull into port at lunchtime and visit a local *taverna* while the boat's cook would buy supplies for dinner. It was peaceful and romantic. I knew so little about boats, however, that when we came home I told people that either the boat was 700 feet long or the cost was $700 a week. (I certainly was having glamorous honeymoons.)

Returning to Chicago, Furth moved into the palace with me, the kids, and the domestic staff. The household was running smoothly, I was doing my work and loving it, and felt I had completed the picture with a Regular Dad in place.

During our marriage, we traveled some, but I remember only two trips specifically. One was to see the Stanley Cup in Canada. (Talk about pearls before swine.) The other was to Israel in 1972, where I had arranged, through Simcha Dinitz, a friend who was Golda Meir's political secretary, to write a series about Israel and its politics for the *Daily News* and my syndicate. Furth was wildly enthusiastic about visiting Israel. He had been there before and was extremely gung ho. I had never been, and I was bowled over by the country's beauty, if put off a little by the breakfasts featuring radishes and other salad fixings. (These people were clearly vegetarians before vegetarianism was cool.) Those were the days when Israeli military personnel were everywhere, and the tradition was for civilian cars to pick up hitchhiking soldiers. Because I was a journalist for whom the government had set up the trip, we had a driver and a translator. I noticed after picking up a few soldiers that they did not speak. I mentioned this to the translator. His feeling was that they felt I was not Jewish, so they thought it best not to say anything. It was then that I learned the only Hebrew I would ever know: "Ani lo shiksa," which means "I am not a shiksa." Then they talked.

Dinitz arranged interviews for me with important Israeli figures in both Jerusalem and Tel Aviv. Among them were Teddy Kollek (then Jerusalem's mayor); Moshe Dayan's daughter, Yael; and David Ben-Gurion. I could not get Dinitz to cough up Golda—and I asked more than once. The answer was always the same: "She sends her best regards."

We were driven to Sde Boker, a kibbutz in the Negev Desert, to see Ben-Gurion. The old gentleman entertained us on his terrace for four hours. I asked how he had first come to Israel. At about the second hour into his answer to this one question, I realized he was not exactly on his game. Furth was a rapt audience, while I was admiring his very handsome bodyguards, counting backward from one hundred, and reviewing who I had to buy gifts for. Ben-Gurion was to die the next year, but alas, when I interviewed him his mind had already begun the departure.

After some months of pleasant domesticity, the fractures in our family framework started to become visible, and sadly, I began to realize that this husband was a mistake, too.

For one thing, he wasn't quite the father figure I had in mind. My hope that the role of stepdad would transition smoothly into that of an involved and loving father-surrogate was a nonstarter.

It was revealed gradually, as we were all living together, that he did not care much for my children, nor they for him. He didn't seem to have much time for them, and I could find no discernible warmth from him to them. And truth be told, I wasn't crazy about his son, either. Children, of course, like dogs (forgive me) sense who likes them and who doesn't, so as far as the Coleman children were concerned, this "dad" wasn't much better than their last one. In my father's phrase, Furth was "showering them with indifference," and they felt it and responded in kind.

I had also hoped that his one child and my three would magically bond—or at least that his son and my son would. Unfortunately, that did not happen either.

As I was to learn firsthand (and later from friends, and later still from my advice-giving career), blended families are not automatically successful. In fact, it is often tough sledding. Every once in a while a remarried couple can get lucky in this regard, but more often than not, everyone is in therapy or competing interests/competing children make things very tense. As a friend said to me, "Nobody really cares about anybody else's children." An ideal blended family *can* happen if the stars are in alignment, but it is nowhere near being a sure thing.

I was hopelessly naïve in thinking that the simple act of bringing a nice man into the fold would create an instant happy family. People with children who decide to remarry should definitely spend time together in all kinds of different circumstances before they finalize their plans, something I neglected to do. Laying this groundwork gives everyone a chance to observe ongoing interactions, eliminating any decisions based solely on everyone being on their best behavior. The kids should have input before a remarriage is a *fait accompli*. The very fact of time put in will reveal relational dynamics that cannot be known when it's just two adults making the decision to marry.

It is not uncommon for people with young children to marry a second time and then wind up divorcing because the new wife or husband does not even come close to managing well with the "new" children. Couples who are serious about their relationship should not, by any means, simply have a few dinners *ensemble* followed by an afternoon with all the kids playing together and then announce they're getting married—which is basically what I did. I made the decision myself that this man would do well with my children. I didn't involve them at all, and the failure to do so became apparent rather quickly as we tried to blend our families and our lives.

In retrospect, I now know I was deciding *for* them what would work, as opposed to taking my time and observing the interactions. As I mentioned previously in this book, when I look back, I realize that my younger self was not inclined to give many decisions the time that is needed to make an educated choice. In my youth, I greatly underestimated the value of *waiting.* Much later, having finally learned that time is a friend, and that faults or unknowns have a hard time remaining hidden forever, I went on to advise everyone—regarding any decision—to, in essence, sleep on it, and for a good long time. I am convinced that many of my own heartbreaks and mistakes could have been avoided if the instant gratification impulse could have been tamped down in favor of proceeding with caution.

Realizing that this marriage wasn't what I'd hoped for began to take its toll on me. I still went through the motions of daily married life, but by year three I had become deeply unhappy. I took a dive and was diagnosed with clinical depression. I was weepy, devoid of energy, mostly sat in a chair and halted my column. My psyche and my body were clearly saying, "This is a mess." And the second one, yet.

A wonderful thing did happen, though, during this desolate period. Early in the Furth era, I had interviewed the acclaimed French mime Marcel Marceau at the French Consulate in Chicago. I did not particularly care for him, probably because he was an egomaniac, but I did warm to his elder brother/minder/ roadie/manager, Alain Mangel (the family name). We somehow communicated with an ease that can occasionally happen when you meet a kindred spirit. I loved that Alain shared some of my unkind feelings about Marcel! He referred to his younger brother and himself as "the oy vey brothers." He tired of his brother's narcissism and demanding nature, and he disdained his "sisters-in-law," which Marcel would collect in various cities where he performed. There was nothing to be done, however, because Alain was the business brains, ran the Mime School in Paris, and managed the bookings. They were inextricably entwined and that was that.

We stayed in touch, and when Marcel performed in New York or Chicago, Alain would let me know and we would get together. As it happened, Alain called during my black cloud period. Marcel was performing at Northwestern University, and Alain wanted to come spend the afternoon with me. I told him that would not be possible because I was crying all the time. He insisted on coming, even after I protested. When I opened the door at his knock, he had a big pot of azaleas and said, "I bring you azalies; I bring you sunshine."

We sat in the library for two hours and he told me about what he did in the French Resistance. Marcel, then, was still a little boy. Alain said nothing in his life had ever equaled the excitement or the feeling of doing something so important. I did not cry the whole time he was there.

We would stay in touch for many years after that and see each other either in the United States or in Paris. However, after some years, the friendship drifted. I learned of his death when I saw Marcel in an American Airlines lounge and asked after Alain. "Ee eze gone," he told me. And to this day azaleas make me think of sunshine, and they always bring to mind Alain.

With pharmaceutical help and a good psychiatrist, I began to understand whence the black cloud came: it found me when I had committed another clunker marriage. In addition to the glued-on-father-in-the-family not working out, I had to acknowledge that he just wasn't bright enough for me. I did not like being the smarter one, having spent my adult life being an intellectual groupie. After the bloom was off the rose I had to face the fact that he bored me.

I remembered a saying of my father's from his early years in the millinery business: "Your first markdown is your cheapest." That is to say, if a hat isn't selling, don't keep marking it down; just slash the price and cut your losses. So that's what I did.

And so it was that in less than four years, stem to stern, I told Furth, in my beautiful gray bedroom, that the marriage wasn't working and that he would need to leave. I regretted that he was so stunned and hurt. To try to make him feel better, I said of course I was returning the ancestral rock, seeing as how it had been in his family for generations and really did not belong to me. I also said he could have Tosh, the family Yorkie. He was so fond of that dog that I thought it would help him through the tough times. He gratefully accepted. When I told the children of my parting gift, however, all three of them said, "But, Mother, that is *our dog*." I said it was the least we could do because Jules was so sad and we must always do what we can to help others feel better.

Then Adam got teary and said my being divorced was hurtful to him. I couldn't believe he was attached to Jules, but...maybe. I asked if he would miss him. No, he said. It was just that with a second divorce the kids in his class would think his mother was nuts, and that is pretty close to a verbatim quote.

Just as with the starter husband, I figured out—after the fact, to be sure—where I had stumbled. In this case I had gone looking, specifically, for a comfortable guy who seemed solid. Such a mate would feel like a relief after Coleman. Obviously I did not know myself very well at the time or acknowledge my need for excitement. Ordinary didn't do it for me. I would advise anyone not to settle—yet that is what I did. Haste makes waste, as the saying goes, and it also makes for bad decisions. My situation with Furth also confirmed for me that a guy doesn't have to be a bum for a woman to want to call it a day.

This was an anxiety-free divorce—except for one aspect. Furth chose his business lawyer as his divorce lawyer, who just happened to be married to my best friend. His partners begged him not to handle the case, but he did. My best guess is that it was a passive-aggressive jab at his wife. Alas, the friendship did not survive.

Once again, my parents were supportive and not terribly sorry to see him go. I think by now I had accustomed them to having a divorced daughter. The roster now was two down: The Prick and The Puck. My wonderful mother, never one to mince words, when asked about the grounds for this divorce would answer simply, "Boredom."

The kids were relieved. And I? What had I learned? For one thing, designer husbands were not the answer. To go looking for someone to fill a slot actually puts the dead hand on falling in love without an agenda in the back of your mind. It also prevents you from seeing all aspects of the relationship. I had wanted a functional father for my kids and miscalculated. By fixating on one thing—in this case, finding a father surrogate—I wound up with tunnel vision. There really is no way to know how a new family dynamic will play out until quite a bit of time has been invested. Alas, the question (again) becomes: What's the hurry?

In this particular case there were no *obvious* impediments. I mean, he was not high-strung, not deeply involved in his business, and blessedly only a social drinker. I was just so overly focused on grafting a "dad" onto our family that I did not take him at face value. It was proof that agendas don't work.

I returned to journalism. This time I went out over the wire, having given up my syndication. Jim Hoge, then-editor of the *Sun-Times*, declared, "Writing is what Margo does between husbands." I pretty much decided I was done with marriage—but I did leave myself some wiggle room. I remember thinking: if I ever do this again, it's going to be for *me*. It would have to be a love match with someone who was brainy, kind and interesting. As for the children, I had to hope that if I were happy, they would be, too.

Furth went on to remarry. I only saw him once after our divorce when a close friend died and her memorial service was at the Furth Chapel. We had a cordial greeting, shook hands, and I felt absolutely nothing.

He died in 2003.

CHAPTER SIX

Wherein a whirlwind romance and love at first sight work really well for many years.

Toward the end of 1976 I was separated from Furth and the kids and I were all doing just fine. Even then (almost 40 years ago!) divorce was pretty common, at least among their school friends' parents, so they did not feel like weird outliers living under the "D" cloud.

By this time, Abra, then 13, was at the Bement School in Massachusetts. That decision had been made unilaterally by her father after she and her friends trashed a hotel suite (in his hotel) celebrating her eighth-grade graduation. I did not protest, as I knew boarding school had been traditional in Coleman's family. Plus, she was a handful.

Happily, there was no tension in the house. There was also no dog. This meant I was easily blackmailed into getting a pair of "racing turtles," Step and Fetchit; Rabbit Redford; a pair of gerbils; and a cat who was somehow more neurotic than most. And I seem to recall a bird that came to a bad end under the dining room table, courtesy of the cat.

Though not yet officially divorced from Furth, we were separated, so I had no compunctions about dating. This was, in a way, same song/second verse, relative to my situation with Coleman when we had separated. I believed (and so advised others, later on) that if a couple is kaput and not living under the same roof, dating is permissible because, in all the ways that count, the marriage is over.

I was dating here and there, and for a time I was seeing a darling guy named Peter Rittmaster who designed small racing yachts. He was in Chicago for a stretch, though his company was based in Miami. Peter had recently been divorced, but his former wife caused me to summon up every bit of self-confidence I could muster, as she was the gorgeous Israeli movie star Daliah Lavi who had been in *Casino Royale*, among other films. Neither Peter nor I was thinking of marriage, but we had a lot of fun together and a lovely romantic friendship.

Around this time I was writing a lot of celebrity profiles, and a publicist asked if I wanted to interview the actor Ken Howard, who was bringing the national tour of *Equus* to Chicago. I had never heard of him, which surprised the publicist, who said he had starred on Broadway, on television and in the movies. What *was* interesting to me was *Equus*. I had seen it in London and thought it so terrific I tried to invest in the American version, but it was closed to investors by the time I made inquiries.

The publicist wanted me to see the play, so the night before I was to do the interview I went to *Equus* with Peter. I thought Ken was enormously talented—and I really *had* never seen him before. After the play, Peter said, in a light-hearted way, that he had a hunch the interview the next day would send me and "Dr. Dysart" (his role in *Equus*) off into the sunset. I have no idea why he made such a statement—though he did turn out to be right.

The interview was arranged so that we would meet at the late morning taping of *Kup's Show, the* TV show for celebrities visiting Chicago. Taping different segments of the show that day were Tom Wolfe and Gene Wilder. During Ken's taping, I paid little attention to what he was saying and instead chatted with Tom Wolfe.

When Ken was finished, I went over to this exceptionally tall blond person and introduced myself. Then we made our way out of the WBBM studios to go to lunch. I had booked it at Cricket's, the chic restaurant named for my youngest child. (It was, of course, in one of her father's hotels.) Walking down the hall to the street, the interview subject looked down at me and asked, "How ya doin'?" Oh, good, I thought, a big, dumb ballplayer.

During the cab ride to the restaurant he was quiet, and I remarked that he seemed down. He confirmed this, saying he'd had "a year of mishaps."

I responded with something my mother often said: "Don't worry, you'll dance again."

He tilted his head and looked at me quizzically. "Why did you mention dancing?"

I told him it was just something we said in our family. As though I had unlocked an emotional door, he started to talk.

His recently departed ladylove had been Donna McKechnie, Broadway's dazzling chorus girl/dancer who was the original Cassie in *A Chorus Line*. She had dumped him to marry Michael Bennett, the show's creator and choreographer—the show's *bisexual* creator and choreographer, who strongly tilted toward male lovers. One could understand why that particular breakup would be depressing.

Arriving at Cricket's, we were shown to a table for two, ordered, and out came my pad and pen. Then it just sort of slipped out that I had not seen any of his work. To my surprise he was charmed—immediately setting him apart from probably everyone else in his line of work. Helping me out, this king-sized John Lindsay look-alike (sort of) told me about himself. He was raised in Manhasset, New York, of course playing basketball in high school, and then going on to play at Amherst College. (He was six foot six.) He loved to sing in school musicals, and left a fellowship at Yale Drama School early when he got a small part on Broadway in *Promises, Promises*. He progressed to being a leading man who sang and danced. (Tommy Tune, another giraffe, taught him to dance.) An irony was that, at age twenty-six, he won a Tony for best supporting actor for his work in *Child's Play*, a straight play. He guessed he was probably best known for playing Thomas Jefferson in *1776*, both on Broadway and in the movie version, and for the two television series he had starred in: *Adam's Rib* and *The Manhunter*.

About an hour and a half into our lunch he said, "Put the pad away." Then we were just two people who'd met and didn't want to stop talking. We soon found that we'd been sitting there for four hours, and by then it was just us and the restaurant staff cleaning up and resetting the tables. Then he said, "Let's go to the Ambassador for an Irish coffee." And so we went to his hotel for what turned into a two-hour coffee. When he said he regretted having to leave to get ready for his performance, he asked if he could see me afterward. I gave him my address and promised to make him an après-theater egg salad sandwich.

After the show, he arrived at my place, got off the elevator on my floor, looked at the eighty-foot-long terrazzo hallway and whistled.

"Be it ever so humble..." I said, and led him into the breakfast room for his "dinner."

We talked nonstop for a couple of hours, and when I said I was tired and thought it was time for bed, he said, "You know, it's been a long day for me, too. Why don't I just crash here?"

"You've got to be kidding," I said, and escorted him to the door.

We made a date for the following night after the play. Then he moved in. So as not to jar the children, I hung his coat in my dressing room instead of the front coat closet. The next day I phoned Rittmaster to tell him his premonition had been right.

It didn't take long for Ken to become a constant presence in my home, and soon enough his coat was hung in the front closet, and the pretense that he went home at night was dispensed with. Adam and Cricket liked him a great deal and welcomed his participation in our family life. And he liked them. (Since Abra was at boarding school, she had not met him yet.) The kids didn't mind the sleeping arrangements, though Adam, the mathematician, calculating the difference between Ken's height and mine, did have a mechanical question about how we were able to "do it." I told him to mind his own business.

To my surprise, the column I'd written about him had the whole town talking. Many journalist friends told me, after the fact, that they'd guessed from what I wrote that Mr. Howard and I would either marry or have a red-hot romance. Truly, when I put that column together, I had no such ideas. In retrospect, people's antennae might have been up because I usually wrote with an edge, whereas this piece was quite friendly. I merely said he looked like the advance man for sex appeal, and speculated that he was what you'd get if you crossed a lion and a poet and sent it to an Ivy League school. The bottom line, figuratively, was that I thought he was a classy guy who was totally without any showbiz grandiosity.

Ours was a love affair that played out in the Chicago media, and a grand romance and courtship it was. He would come home after his show and reheat whatever the kids and I had had for dinner, usually improving it. We would sleep late and usually spend the day together, save for matinee days. Sometimes I would go to the theater in the evening and camp out in his dressing room. I really did love this routine. Theatrical companies were like families, and his cast and crew were most welcoming.

Plus, I was madly and deeply in love—perhaps for the first time. It would be fair to say that this was the great romance of my life. To be in your thirties and find "the one perfect other," as we used to tell each other, is very special. There is a vigor and an electricity when you are still young that is not duplicable, say, when you're in your fifties. You can be crazy about someone in your fifties and on up, but it ain't like being in your thirties. We relished the good times and knew how lucky we were. Sometimes, apropos of nothing in particular, Ken would say, "We beat 'em." We just didn't think people could be this happy.

Almost everyone talked about how gorgeous he was. I suppose I knew this to be true, but it was not a major attraction for me. His looks were almost an anomaly in my life, considering some of the men I'd been with. A few of them had been good looking, but that was never what did it for me, as I've mentioned before. Intellect and humor were my aphrodisiacs, except when I unfortunately made an exception for Mr. Right #2. (As for the starter husband, intellect he had, as well as dry humor, but that whole setup was so skewed as to wind up outside of the realm of rationality as it related to my life.) More affecting to me was listening to Ken talk. I have always loved a beautiful male voice, perhaps because words and language were the coin of my realm.

While in town, he was the celebrity in residence. He hosted the Chicago Emmys and entertained at a few charity events. At one he sang, "Just in Time." (He was, by then, known to New York theatergoers as a song-and-dance man, primarily from *1776* and *Seesaw*.) I can think of few things more romantic than having a song sung to you in a public setting.

My younger kids, however—Adam, in particular—regarded this new man as someone who'd basically come to town with the circus, since their idea of what men did for a living came from their financier father. Sensing (correctly) that this man might become permanent, Adam confronted him one day in the kitchen.

"So, when're you gonna settle down and go into business?" the eleven-year-old asked.

Ken said he would think about that.

It was almost unheard of to keep a touring company in Chicago for six months, but Ken and company did it with *Equus*. One night after the show, we came home and opened the front door. As we walked in Ken looked up and down the runway that was my front hall and said, "Let me take you away from all this." And that was his proposal.

I laughed, because of course that line usually suggested rescue from a rather simple, small dwelling, and also, by then, it was a *fait accompli* that we would be together and that I would leave Chicago when he did. Maybe because of the children, we knew we would marry, or maybe it was because we wanted to. Nothing was going to be better than this.

Happily, my mother was thrilled. I suspect my father might have been, too, except that he was in London, remarried to a woman six years my junior, and we were estranged.

Ken and I became officially engaged on Christmas Eve. My gift to him was a gold keychain with an engraved disc saying, "I owe the horse a lot." His gift to me was a gold ring with a diamond buckle. I asked him what *kind* of ring it was. He laughed and said it was a "friendship ring." Then, I asked him, "Well, what *kind* of ring did you ask for when you went to buy it?" This conversation got me nowhere.

I didn't need to ask any more questions, however, when not too many days later he asked for a ring of mine that fit the fourth finger of the left hand. Then he went to Tiffany's and bought a diamond eternity band, which we stashed in a safe in my bedroom closet—not to be retrieved until March 13, 1977. That day, we were married after the mid-afternoon Sunday matinee in front of the lions at the Art Institute under a tree.

Joel Flaum, a friend of mine who was a federal judge, officiated. My witness was another federal judge, my dear friend Ilana Rovner. Ken's best man was the young actor who played "the boy" in *Equus*, Achilles Massahos. We wanted the wedding ceremony itself to be bare bones—just enough attendants to be legal. No kids, no parents, no friends other than those who were part of the wedding.

However, the party started afterward, when we five went to a favorite French restaurant we'd taken over for the night. Everyone who was invited assumed it was an engagement party. When Ken made his divine toast saying we had just been married, there was whooping and cheering and everyone was genuinely surprised— including my mother, whose nose was the tiniest bit out of joint— though Ken did inform her before he made the toast. I had major help planning the evening from an artistically inclined, organizationally adept crew member traveling with the show. The wedding cake was a tall croquembouche tower. Lots of friends, along with many media people, shared that warm and wonderful evening with us, celebrating our four-and-a-half-month whirlwind courtship.

When news of our marriage was published and I was identi-fied as a journalist, Peter Stone, the great Broadway wit and writer of, among other shows, *1776*, sent a telegram: "Good for you! I hear she gives good headline."

And Mr. Right #2 wrote a gracious note: "You are going to do it until you get it right. Best wishes, Jules."

Mr. Coleman, I can only guess, was furious, because he phoned me the next day to declare that my marriage was "tacky." I was somewhat taken aback because he'd had no unpleasant remarks about my second marriage. I could only deduce that he felt outclassed. And I actually felt a little sorry for him. His former wife's new husband was six foot six, handsome, blond and talented. And not Jewish. Draw your own conclusions.

Just weeks after we married, I had a minor surgical proce-dure that kept me in the hospital for two nights. *Equus* was still running, and Ken would come to see me after the curtain came down. This offered a preview of coming attractions regarding rules and perks if you were a heartthrob actor. The nurses were beside themselves with excitement, totally ignoring visiting hours (which, of course, had ended much earlier) and behaving like a brigade of fans in starched white caps. He would get in bed with me, and we would catch up about the performance and what was going on at home. He was devoted and adorable, what can I tell you?

When Abra came home for Christmas vacation, it was inter-esting to watch her gigolo-ize Ken, calling him "daaaahling." All I could figure out was that, to her mind, his good looks and being four years younger than I made him undeserving of respect. (They would eventually become friends, but it was tough going at first.) Adam was over the moon that this lovely man who had "married" us actually enjoyed spending time with him, and of course they both loved to shoot hoops! Cricket, quite shy and rather cool to me, came out of her shell in response to his warmth and attention. Son of a gun. I had said the next one was for me, if there *was* a next one, yet he turned out to be a gift to my children.

And my mother was crazy about him. Just as she had changed her mind about divorce when I unloaded Coleman, so she now rethought her position on "mixed marriages" when I found this lovely First Congregationalist—a man who had warmth, smarts, generosity, the works. Ken and I called each other baby-talk names, like fools, and I could hardly believe, at the age of thirty-seven, with three kids and two divorces on my resume, that I was insanely happy, married to a man who came to regard my children as his own. And he never, ever used the word *stepchildren*.

I found it admirable that he managed to be so optimistic in a business I would go on to learn was loaded with rejection. Perhaps he had this outlook because he was talented—and lucky. There is a line from *The Little Foxes* that he said often: "I'm lucky, Horace. I've always been lucky; I'll be lucky again." He'd won his Tony at the age of twenty-six, and, after that, he'd won pretty much all the other theater awards. Ken had a home on the New York stage, but "settling down and going into business" pretty much dictated that we would move to Hollywood.

And so it was that he started asking friends to look into schools for Adam and Cricket and told his agents at William Morris to rustle up something for when he was done with *Equus*. When the show did finally close, we hung around Chicago, I put the apartment on the market, and we waited for him "to go into business." People thought I was "so brave" to leave Chicago and the palace, but I didn't give it a second thought. The person who I thought *was* brave was Ken. He was four years younger than I and was walking into a ready-made family. Although he had been married previously for two years to the actress Louise Sorel, there were no children. (And interestingly, she, too, was Jewish and four years older than he was.)

The first project that came Ken's way was a Movie of the Week about the Super Bowl called *Superdome*. We decamped to New Orleans for the six-week shoot, and that was some introduction to "the business" for me: Ken's cast mates were David Janssen, Edie Adams, Van Johnson, Donna Mills, Tom Selleck, Dick Butkus, Bubba Smith and a gaggle of professional football players! I found Bubba to be a sweet man — but perhaps less so after I heard that, when he played, people would yell from the stands, "Kill, Bubba. Kill." We spent a lot of time with Selleck, who was recently separated from his wife and hardly known then. He'd just finished a pilot but worried that having been the Salem cigarette man on billboards would hurt him. At that time it was déclassé to do ads and commercials if you were "a real actor." (That was of course, to change.) I found him to be a comfortable guy and good company. Oh, and his pilot *was* picked up. It was *Magnum, P.I.*

I was the perfect civilian wife for someone in the movie business. I was a hotel rat and had been since I was young. In the beginning I was on the set every day to watch how the sausage was made. It really was a lot of fun. Film sets have their own language. *Craft services* are food. The *best boy* is a man who is second in command to the key grip (lighting). Historically, that title came from the director who said, "Give me your best boy." The *DP* is director of photography (cinematographer). The *martini* is the last shot of the day, and the *Abby Singer* is the second-to-last. I actually would meet Abby Singer, who worked for MTM, about a year after the shoot in New Orleans. And the best source of gossip is the Teamster drivers.

When that shoot was over, we returned to Chicago to arrange for the move to Los Angeles. When Coleman got wind of this, he made fast arrangements to put *all* the children in boarding school. Cricket, then ten years old, was about to enter fifth grade and was clearly too young, although she thought it would be fun. Adam, who was eleven and a half, was too young as well, and he vocally and bitterly protested that he did not want to go. He'd always had a precocious sense of who had the power and railed against the fact that, as a little boy, it was not him.

I will say this for Coleman: he knew how to pick elite schools. Cricket's pre-prep school was the North Country School in Lake Placid, New York, for grades four through nine. There was a three to one student-to-teacher ratio, and many of its ninety students were the children of diplomats, theater people or die-hard boarding school disciples. North Country was an early adherent to healthy eating, so there was no white flour and no refined sugar. (I found it ironic that one of Cricket's buddies there was the child of the family who owned the Palm Restaurants.)

The school selected for Adam was the Eaglebrook School for grades six through nine, in Deerfield, Massachusetts. It was the feeder school to Deerfield Academy. Adam went there kicking and screaming, but he came to love it, and that school made him a star, both academically and in sports.

No doubt as a response to his father's wealth and the behavior that went with it, Adam became hostile to money, which made Eaglebrook problematic. He would show his disdain by referring to his schoolmates by the names of their families' businesses. I remember KitchenAid and Fiat. And there were the two brothers he identified as "Jordans." These were sons of the "little" King Hussein of Jordan. (Their mother was Princess Muna, born a British commoner who should have been acceptable to Adam because she worked as a secretarial assistant on the film set of *Lawrence of Arabia*.) The princes, of course, came with security, but at least they were low key, lived in a local motel, and wore casual clothes. Dean Witter, J. Press and Firestone complicated Adam's calculated rudeness because their actual names were the same as the family business.

Anyway, he solved his rich-kid problem by choosing to room with someone without a famous name and who didn't strike him as preppy. That turned out to be his buddy Myles, a black classmate from Harlem whose father was an NBC cameraman. And seeing as how they are friends to this day, it was obviously a good choice. Parents' weekends were a hoot. James Baker was part of this rarified PTA, as was Elizabeth Taylor, because John Warner III was a student. No King Hussein, however. (And now, Abdullah, one of the "Jordans," is King.)

There were a few things at play in this boarding school drama. I knew Coleman was trying to stick it to me, but I still felt overpowered by him and unable to fight back. On a semi-unconscious, lower frequency was the realization that being in a new marriage in a new town would be easier if I did not have day-to-day obligations to the children. Now, with all of them away at school, we were off to California. Ken decided we would live in Pacific Palisades in West Los Angeles, the family-oriented community for movie people. Walter Matthau was the honorary mayor.

The first house we rented was in Will Rogers Park, not far from the polo field. (Will Rogers liked to play polo, and some movie people still play.) Ken loved to hike in that area, and he'd set off in the morning with a lunch packed by Lulu, my house-keeper from Chicago. I had not run a house on my own since the early years of my first marriage, and I had no confidence I could do so now. I'm sure it looked a little peculiar that a young couple would bring a housekeeper to a modest house, but there you are.

Ken figured out the best way to settle down and go into business was to create a television series for himself. His close buddy from Amherst College, David E. Morine (always referring to himself by his full name), suggested that Ken put together a television series that would recreate his own Manhasset High School basketball career, where he had been the only white starter on an all-black team and was, in fact, called "The White Shadow." He would play his actual coach from those years.

Bruce Paltrow was a longtime friend because his wife, Blythe Danner, had often been paired with Ken on Broadway, television, and at the Williamstown Theatre Festival in Massachusetts. They had been a stage couple for quite some time. A lot of people just assumed there had to have been a romance, but Ken told me this was not the case. I did, however, wonder whether this was true at the beginning of one Williamstown season; when Blythe spotted him, she came racing over, jumped into his arms and wrapped her legs around his waist. This bespoke previous intimacy to me, but maybe it was an exuberant, showbiz kind of greeting. Who knows.

In any case, when Ken was figuring out how to put together *The White Shadow*, nothing much was happening for Bruce at the time, and without knowing it, Ken handed him a career. He told him the outline of the story he thought could be a series and asked him to write the pilot. They therefore owned the show and took it to CBS, where it was green-lighted. Part of the conceit of the story was that the coach, "Ken Reeves," had been an NBA player who was cut due to injuries. For a convincing backstory, they needed a real NBA team for which the character, Coach Reeves, would have played. One of the producers got in touch with the LA Lakers' office and asked if they could film half a day with Ken on their bench, showing some of the Lakers as his teammates. The answer was yes—for a payment of $100,000. CBS was not going to sail for this, so they were stuck as to how to rope in a major team—for no money.

I never imagined I would become involved in the business end of Ken's career, but I thought I could solve this particular problem. My parents were friends of Marge and Everett Kovler in Chicago. Although the family's business was Jim Beam, their son, Jon Kovler, was managing partner of the Chicago Bulls, so I called him and explained the situation. He immediately understood the publicity advantage of having the Bulls referenced on a prime-time TV show, and he laughed about the Lakers wanting 100 large, saying, "Stuff your pockets with $100 bills and that will secure releases from any players you film." CBS was skittish about sending the star, his wife, Paltrow, Jackie Cooper (the director) and a second unit crew to Chicago on the say-so of Ken Howard's wife . . . but they did it. And it worked. Hundred dollar bills all around, and there was Coach Reeves, the injured Chicago Bull, sitting on the bench with players like Tate Armstrong, Artis Gilmore, and a whole bunch of other people I'd never heard of.

The show was filmed at MTM Studios. Grant Tinker was then married to Mary Tyler Moore, and one of our producers was his son, Mark. No TV show focusing on sports had ever succeeded before. But in addition to being a great success, *The White Shadow* was the first ensemble drama in prime-time TV with a predominantly black cast.

With three seasons and fifty-four episodes, it ordinarily would not have qualified for syndication, but it was considered so special it was syndicated anyway. Newt Minow of the Federal Communications Commission (FCC), who famously bemoaned the general junk on TV, naming it "the vast wasteland," loved *The White Shadow*. As did William Paley—longtime chairman of CBS, who was coincidentally from Manhasset, Ken's hometown. The show had wildly enthusiastic fans who surprised us by knowing every episode and having favorite characters. Frank Sinatra could go into great detail about *The White Shadow*. So could Andrew Young during his stint as an ambassador to the United Nations. When he mentioned this to us, we were both curious as to how he found the time to watch a television series.

This show was the rocket that launched Ken into TV stardom. He'd had the lead in a few previous series (one with Blythe) but nothing had caught fire like *The White Shadow*. There is a long shelf life for stars with a hit series—future series, Movies of the Week, miniseries, you name it.

My work was portable, which was fortunate, because we were always together for the first ten years, and many things were shot on location away from LA. Although the editor of the *Los Angeles Herald-Examiner*, Jim Bellows (who had bought my syndicated column some years earlier), invited me to work for him, LA was not my town and my new life precluded "a real job." What I did do was become a magazine freelancer for a most incongruous list of publications. It all had to do with which editors liked my work.

(At a party in New York I was introduced to the celebrated *New Yorker* writer Brendan Gill with this preface: "Margo's a writer, too." *Oh, God,* I thought, *please don't let him pursue this.* But Gill duly asked for whom I wrote. It was, let us say, a diverse mixture: the *New Republic, People, The Nation, Good Housekeeping, TV Guide* and *Newsday.*)

We left Will Rogers Park after about a year for a house on Toyopa Drive, with Walter and Carol Matthau diagonally across the street. I had interviewed Walter a few years earlier in Chicago, so it was fun to be reacquainted with this disheveled, funny man. (He actually scandalized me during the interview, for about a minute, when he told me he had to sit at a piano bench, nude, for a movie—though of course the audience would never see his privates. Nonetheless, he told me he feared a wayward shot, recording for posterity "his shriveled-up old mushroom." Oh, my.)

There was something interesting to me about Los Angeles real estate. It was all about who had lived there before—even if it was John Barrymore in the 1930s. We rented the Toyopa house from Bobby Vinton, "The Polish Prince" who was known for singing "Blue Velvet." Ken promised me one zip code (the Palisades) but said he never wished to own a house in California. He was, to a degree, conflicted about "the business," and never fully committed to the work or the town. As he once articulated, it boiled down to his questioning why a guy who'd gone to Amherst and Yale was wearing makeup and putting on costumes.

With *The White Shadow* he became famous and instantly recognizable. While I was somewhat accustomed to this because of my mother, the manifestation of the adulation was different. When Mother's fans greeted her, it was with thanks for smart and useful advice, for the social stands she took and for her helpfulness to millions. Of course they were thrilled to meet a celebrity they admired, but no one ever said, after shaking hands with her, "I will never wash this hand again." Nor did they get so excited that they said garbled things like, "You're my biggest fan." My favorite was the man outside a deli in Lake Placid who said, "You know, you look just like Ken Howard!"

Ken said, "Well, that's who I am."

And the man said, "No, no, but you really look like him."

One thing Ken did escape, probably because of his imposing height and physique, was that people did not attempt to touch him or try to make off with a piece of his clothing. My only difficulty being annexed to a television star was that I never did know what to say when people would ask me, after securing his autograph, "Are you anybody?"

I never heard the movie people we knew overtly make fun of the fans, but I'm pretty sure the feeling was there. It just seemed silly for people to seem so worshipful or to wait hours so they could see an actor enter an event. A Hollywood luminary was a performer, after all, not the Dalai Lama. Ken, however, was friendly and gracious to fans, signing autographs and posing for pictures. But not everyone was. I remember an A-list actor barking a forceful, "No!" at a 12-year-old kid who asked for an autograph. Maybe it all boiled down to what H. L. Mencken observed: "A celebrity is one who is known to many persons he is glad he doesn't know."

I only slipped into fan mode once, having met too many public figures over the years to be star struck. Having behaved normally when meeting or spending an evening with people like Paul Newman, Robert Redford, Clint Eastwood, Michael Caine, Warren Beatty, or Jack Nicholson, et al, I confess to walking by

Peter O'Toole's table in a restaurant and going, well, "gaga" would not be too strong a word. Ken had preceded me out of the restaurant to have the car brought around, and as I was leaving I spied O'Toole and stopped dead in my tracks in front of his table to make this thoughtful and sophisticated declaration: "Oh, my, it's you." He smiled, was more than gracious, asked me for my name and introduced me to his male companion. He seemed to take my behavior for the compliment it was. Afterward, I could not believe I had done that. Not long after, I saw Christina Pickles, an English actress, and told her of my fan-girl episode.

"We were at the Royal Academy of Dramatic Arts together, and you should have seen him before he climbed into the bottle," she said.

Many of our social friends were in the business because, mostly, that's who you met, either from working together or from parties. And these people were fans in the good way, admiring each other's work, but as peers. They were more or less equals, without any illusions of "glamour." Which is not to say that younger actors were immune from old crushes dating back to when the veteran actors were young. A sweet story illustrating this was when Ken played the German diplomat in *The Thornbirds* in 1983. He had a scene with Jean Peters, whom he had loved from afar as a teenager. When they were ready to roll, he was so excited that he was actually working with this goddess that he fluffed his lines. Peters, somehow understanding where this was coming from, said, "Thank you."

Satellite spouses quickly adapted to socializing with people they had previously only seen on screen or in magazines. When school vacations rolled around, my kids became Hollywood kids—but with a Midwestern sensibility. Adam, with his distaste for displays of wealth, would lie down on the floor of the limousine if we had to take one, and Cricket would say to him, "Get up. No one knows who you are." One of Adam's chums in Los Angeles was Brian Medavoy, a son of the studio head Mike Medavoy. This kid's conversation was all about layoff deals, points, deal memos and other Hollywood terms of art. He also let me know, the first time I met him, that his family was going to spend Christmas with Robert Redford in Aspen. (Another Hollywood kid gave Adam some number by which he could charge long-distance phone calls to Burt Reynolds! When I learned about this I told him he had to cut it out because he could go to jail.) For the kids and me, this new life was very definitely reminiscent of Dorothy in *The Wizard of Oz* saying, "Toto, I have a feeling we're not in Kansas anymore." But as the saying goes, you can get used to anything.

My personality, along with my newspaper training, was to be an observer. This, of course, colored how I was seeing my new life. I would write about the cult of celebrity for the *New Republic*, calling the phenomenon "Celebridrek." The favors, perks and adoration accorded the celebrated were so out of whack as to be disturbing. Even when I was the beneficiary of special handling, I always knew there was something wrong, if not silly, about the fawning flattery elicited by the Famous Face. When I traveled with my mother, a special services agent always escorted her onto the plane, carrying her hand luggage. When I traveled with Ken, beginning in *The White Shadow* years, it was even more over-the-top. An airline captain once walked out of the cockpit before take-off to tell Ken what an honor it was to have him on board! Even as the smiling consort I found it ridiculous being fished out of lines at movie theatres in Westwood to be invited in as "guests" of the management, or being whisked into sold-out restaurants because a Famous Face was considered value added. The irony was not lost on me when I remembered, years earlier, dining with Jonas Salk in Chicago, and he went totally unrecognized in the restaurant we were in—yet just as we were leaving, Tab Hunter appeared…and of course he was mobbed. Jesus, one guy eliminated polio, while the other one was emoting on the silver screen.

For our first Christmas as a new family, the children were to share their school vacation with us and their father. Our holiday was first. The three kids and Ken and I went to Aspen to ski—the kids' choice. (Clearly not mine. I tried to ski once, fell down, broke a nail and that was that.) When we returned to California after a week, the children were to join Coleman in Vail. However, all three kids said they didn't want to join their father, and Ken and I agreed they shouldn't be forced to do so. A few months later, Coleman sued us for custody. It was pretty clear that the embarrassment of his children choosing not to see him—with houseguests as witnesses to the snub—is what triggered the suit. Not to mention that the children's new and beloved stepfather was the same six foot six tall, blond, wicked handsome Christian man who had impelled Coleman to call and tell me my marriage was "tacky." Only now, this man was a hero to America's children, courtesy of a hit television show. That had to be hard, and clearly served as the catalyst to get Coleman's competitive juices flowing.

We were horrified by the custody suit and told the children of this development. They were stunned, fearing they could actually wind up with him. Adam, almost 13 and totally disgusted, phoned his father and said, "I heard what you did, and as far as I'm concerned you're not my father anymore." That was a conversation I shall never forget, and not just for its brevity. Five minutes later Coleman called *me*, hollering the question: "You actually told them?" I said it would be pretty dumb to keep it from three kids that they might be removed from their mother's custody. He told me he assumed it would be "just between us."

I knew immediately who I wanted to represent me: Sam Skinner, a Sidley Austin partner who had been the US Attorney in Chicago and was known to be a barracuda. (Skinner, later on, would become George H. W. Bush's Secretary of Transportation.) I also wanted someone who was not only top drawer but also someone who knew Coleman, because to know him was to . . . well, never mind. I did not find out until after the fact that the Sidley executive committee had to convene to permit Skinner to represent me because, like so many law firms in America, they had previously represented Coleman. Two partners on the committee, Newt Minow and Mossy Leibman, were friends of my parents and of mine. They also knew Coleman. The decision was that the firm could represent me.

The negotiations dragged on for months. There were court appearances—in Chicago—with more than one "emergency motion" involving the children. At one of these gatherings Coleman's lead lawyer, Don Reuben (the lawyer for my first employer, the *Tribune*, who for all I know was vetting my columns), suggested that the children spend their summer vacation at the Menninger Clinic to find out why they didn't like their father. I am not making this up. Even the bailiffs gasped at the outrageousness of that statement. Then came the *pièce de résistance*.

Skinner's extremely competent and effective second chair, Arlene Erlebacher, addressed the court. From a transcript dated May 4, 1979, she said:

> *Specifically in order to take as little time of the Court, I think I can summarize this quite neutrally to say the basic allegations which are undisputed in this Petition are that the Colemans were once married; they had three children; they have been divorced for eight or nine years. Mr. Coleman claims that initially he had a good relationship with the children; that recently that relationship has ended; that the children no longer show any affection toward him, and refuse to visit him or talk to him.*

> *There seems to be some suggestion, though not an outright allegation in the Petition, that Mrs. Howard's remarriage to Ken Howard, and the fact that he is a television star, has something to do with this, although we are not told what.... But what I would like to bring the Court's attention to is a rather spectacular "Wherefore" clause on the last page.*

> *What Mr. Coleman is now asking this Court is no longer for psychiatric assistance in resolving the visitation problem; rather, he is asking to take these children away from their mother, not to give them to him, but to give them to some neutral third party as a custodian so they would be put in a position to be visited by both parents.*

*They wouldn't live with either parent. They wouldn't
see Mr. Howard, with whom they have established
a relationship.*

*Alternatively, they suggest that the Court order
Margo to leave her husband, Ken Howard, and
move back to Chicago... Apparently they don't
care what the psychiatrist says or whatever you
say. Instead, they want to take these children
away and put them in some neutral institution.
Either that or break up the Howard marriage.*

*The point I am making is Mr. Coleman's attorneys
are well aware, and Mr. Coleman is aware that
this problem in visitation arose last year when
Mr. Coleman filed what I call a spurious custody
Petition. He claimed he had nothing to do with it;
that his then attorneys, Rinella and Rinella, had
filed it without his permission. If you will notice,
this is also not signed by Mr. Coleman.*

*I have asked his attorneys if Mr. Coleman is aware
of it. They say he is, although he is not here to
so state.*

*In addition, your honor, when he filed the last one,
he initially claimed to know nothing about it. And
then he later came up with the excuse that at the
time he was either on drugs or had a hormonal
problem and didn't know what he was doing.*

At this point, his lawyer told the court that my lawyer was "emo-tionally disturbed."

Later on in the proceedings Adam told the court he "didn't love" his father; Cricket said she "just wasn't comfortable" with him; and Abra said, "He just doesn't tell me the truth."

Ken was deposed. Coleman apparently misled his lawyers about who, exactly, he was, because they began the deposition as though they were dealing with a louche rock star who was not particularly educated or familiar with the social graces. In other words: a showbiz bum. The lawyers were at a great loss when the deposition got underway. They asked if he'd gone to school. Yes, he said. Did he graduate? Well, yes. From where? Amherst College. Um, any further schooling? Yes, graduate school at the Yale School of Drama. The lawyers changed their tack, and to make a long deposition short, they ended up ask-ing Ken if he felt he could perhaps teach Coleman how to be a better father.

Things were not looking so good for Mr. Coleman on the custody front, and eventually their side withdrew the action and agreed that the children could decide to see or not see their father as they wished.

Coleman eventually told others, but never me, that this suit was the biggest mistake of his life. None of the children were talking to him afterward, and one particular lasting result of that hideous episode is that Adam took the name Adam Coleman Howard out of respect and affection for the man who was his functional father. And he was very clever about it, I must say. All this was going on while he was at Eaglebrook, where he realized he was known as Adam Coleman, so he waited until he went on to Hotchkiss, in 1981, to ask his new headmaster if he might use the name he preferred, although there had been no formal adoption. That smart man said yes.

The custody suit was the only dark cloud to cross our sky. We had a great romance within our marriage and a helluva lot of fun. He was a great one for leaving love notes—sometimes just a line, like, "I loves you, girl." And I loved that his signature was always the letter *K* made to look like a stick figure song-and-dance man with a top hat and cane.

With the estrangement of the children from their father after he was handed his teeth in that unfortunate court fight, I no longer had to defer to Coleman on matters related to the children, so Ken and I became the de facto parents. Our first decision was to try to undo the damage of everyone being shipped off to boarding school and to let them choose where they wanted to be. As it happened, all three kids had now aged out of their original boarding schools and were now in prep school—or high school, as it is known to most people. Abra was at The Masters School in Dobbs Ferry, New York; Adam was at Hotchkiss in Connecticut; and Cricket was at the Buxton School in Massachusetts. Much to our surprise, the two younger ones decided a better education was to be had on the East Coast, and they opted to stay where they were. Abra, then 16, elected to join us in California and attend a huge public high school, "Pali High." This was the school immortalized by class members Michael Medved and David Wallechinsky in their 1976 book, *What Really Happened to the Class of '65?*

Although Coleman's access to the children did change, his financial obligations to them did not, and getting him to pay bills remained a struggle. Stuart Chase, the estimable headmaster at

Eaglebrook, sent Ken and me a copy of a dunning letter to John sent in October 1979. It began with this:

> *Dear John,*
> *Perhaps the letters from the business office haven't*
> *gotten through to you, but I do want to bring to*
> *your attention that your account with us for Adam*
> *is long overdue.*

Chase added his own note to us in our copy:

> *Dear Ken and Margo: I remember well your*
> *assurances of last year and I dearly hope that John*
> *will take care of this matter honorably and quickly*
> *and we will not have to fall back on you folks...*
>
> *Needless to say, we are worried about this*
> *obligation particularly since the account is the*
> *largest outstanding at this point and I have*
> *a Board of Trustees meeting coming up this Friday.*

And that is how Ken Howard and I became the bank so that John Coleman's children would be allowed to stay in school. And poor Adam was reminded, on occasion, that Coleman had promised Eaglebrook an athletic field and he was asked to please check on the status of the promised gift.

By this time we were renting a beautiful house in the Riviera section of Los Angeles, or as Ken called it, the Olive Oil District.

Our street was Napoli Drive, with the neighboring streets having names like Amalfi and Spezia. The house overlooked the fourth hole at the Riviera Country Club. Like a cemetery, a country club is usually a wonderfully quiet place at night—except, perhaps in California, when there is a convention of coyotes who for some reason choose to meet almost every night. One thing was for sure. In Chicago my neighbors would not have been Dean Martin, William Shatner, Adam West, The Captain & Tennille, Rod Serling's widow, or the very compassionate Dom DeLuise.

DeLuise's good heart was shown one year when Adam was home for some reason on Halloween, and he went door to door trick-or-treating, taking the dog along. Abra rescued this dog, which was part German Shepherd, part wolf. She did this, mind you, while we were out of town. She called my *mother* for permission, who said yes, by all means, yes, get the dog. (This from a woman who referred to everyone's pets as "livestock.") In her honor Abra named the dog Ali, utilizing the initials A and L for Ann Landers, the enabler. I must say, this was my favorite dog ever. The dog's preferred turf was patrolling the deck off Abra's second-floor bedroom. However, she would go berserk when the helicopters flew low and near the deck when President and Mrs. Reagan were in town. (They were neighbors, as well.)

Anyway, when DeLuise opened his door on that fateful Halloween, the dog stepped in and peed in his front hall. He said, "Oh, don't give it a thought," which certainly would not have been my response.

It was with Ken's prodding that I wrote my first book, *Eppie: The Story of Ann Landers*. He was most supportive of my work and herded me into the pool house to write. It was a multi-generational family memoir about my maternal grandparents from Russia, my parents, Mother's troublesome twin, and myself. The book created a stir because it was the direct opposite of *Mommie Dearest*. It was on many local bestseller lists. Mother thought I was far too open about many things and too hard on her twin sister—a sentiment I did not entirely believe. I essentially said goodbye to my Aunt Popo with that book because, although my mother would never answer her calumnies in public, I did. What Mother loved, even with my being too frank, in her opinion, was that so many people told her, and Liz Smith wrote: "If only I had a daughter who could write such a tender, affectionate book."

It was in 1981 that Ken proved to be ahead of the curve of actors wanting to have homes outside of California for when they weren't working. Because Adam was at Hotchkiss in a beautiful part of northwest Connecticut, Ken felt that should be the place. Cricket's school was in Williamstown, Massachusetts, not so far away. (She would go on to Vassar, also proximate.) We bought a beautiful farm in Falls Village, Connecticut. It was on sixty-five acres, abutted the Appalachian Trail, had a waterfall as well as a pond and, after we moved in, a putting green.

Though I was a city girl, through and through, I did grow to love that bucolic life. However, I admit that on our first morning waking up in the house, I did ask Ken, at roughly 6:00 a.m., to turn off the birds; and while he was at it to please tell the bullfrogs to pipe down as well. After a while I even loved looking at what I called my Budget Rent A Cows: a dairy herd belonging to our neighbor, Farmer Twing, who had been using one of our meadows for forever. The house itself was built in 1800, and Ken redid the big red barn to be a gym, a billiard room, a "hers" closet and a caretaker's apartment. We called it "Shadow Farms," because, of course, it was the house that CBS bought.

Ken's presence was well known in the area, and when we were in residence we were invited to galas for various summer theaters in our part of Connecticut. I remember one at the estate of Lewis Mumford's widow. I'd been told she was devoted to maintaining the great writer's legacy, so when I was introduced to her I wanted to acknowledge her late husband's importance. Unfortunately, along with my "gift" for spur-of-the-moment observations fast-tracked from brain to mouth, I also had a talent for cross-pollinating information.

I blurted upon being introduced to her, "Who among us didn't love *Alice in Wonderland*?"

"Well—yes…" she said, with a bemused look.

When Ken and I moved on he said to me, "I think you have confused her late husband with Lewis Carroll."

We had a ton of wonderful experiences, sometimes star-studded, sometimes not, but the fun was that we were together. We went to Israel as part of the "Peretz 14" when Marty was given an honorary degree by Hebrew University. In our posse were friends like his then-wife, Anne; Yo-Yo Ma; Ginny and Roger Rosenblatt (he the longtime literary editor of the *New Republic*); and Nitza and Henry Rosovsky (he the dean of the faculty of arts and sciences at Harvard). Because of Marty's deeply held Zionist beliefs and his ownership of the *New Republic*, to be in Israel with him was like being a guest of the government. Museum entry fees were waived and we partied with people like Teddy Kollek, the illustrious mayor of Jerusalem from 1965 to 1993 who was said to be "the greatest builder of Jerusalem since Herod." My friend Simcha Dinitz, then Golda Meir's political secretary, preceding

his becoming Israel's Ambassador to the United States, entertained for us…with Shimon Peres and Yitzhak Rabin among the
guests. We were in tall cotton, as they say in the South.

During the summer of 1982, four-fifths of our family were at
the Williamstown Theatre Festival in Massachusetts, considered
by many performers and theatergoers to be the top of the line in
summer theater. It was also a theatrical home away from home
for Ken. The eminence there was Nikos Psacharopoulos, who'd
been one of his teachers at Yale Drama School (along with Stella
Adler). Respected actors from the stage vied to be on the main
stage there—as they still do. Nikos's pets during that period were
Ken, Blythe Danner, and Christopher Reeve—who had been an
apprentice years earlier. Nikos was so partial to this trio that the
festival picked up their housing bills, whereas other performers paid
their own way or stayed in Williams College dorms. Abra, being
older (she was twenty at the time), chose to work in Chicago, so
only Adam and Cricket were with us. Adam was in the apprentice
program for acting, and Cricket—who would rather run a forklift
blindfolded than be on a stage—was Chris Reeve's "assistant." She
was fifteen then. He had already played Superman, but she was
not impressed. And Adam actually stole his girlfriend, a wonderful
stage actress named Laila Robins. She was twenty-three, Adam was
seventeen, and Superman was not amused. My problem with Reeve
was that he constantly talked about his "craft," totally glossing over
the fact that his looking so much like the comic book character, not
his "craft," is what greatly helped secure the part of Superman for
him. I also had a mad-on for him when he told my children that
their stepfather was lazy and not fully committed to the business.

Adam was drawn to Ken's profession, so for him spending
time in Williamstown was more than just a way to kill a summer.

When home from school, he would hang out on *The White Shadow* set and pepper everyone with questions, mostly the camera crew. I shouldn't have been surprised when he decided to make the movie business his career, as the kid was always a bit of a fabulist and storyteller. To try to distance himself further from his father's wealth, he would tell people who did not know us that he was one of twelve children from a family who was on food stamps.

In 1984 we were in Dallas where Ken was filming another Movie of the Week, *He's Not Your Son,* costarring with Donna Mills. We were locked up in a Doubletree Hotel where the windows did not open—I guess to preserve the air conditioning. The cast and crew of *Dallas* were camped out there at that time as well. When a movie company puts a lot of people in a hotel, they pay for the rooms and the actors pay their own incidental charges (phones, room service, laundry). Since I was the designated business person in this marriage, I would pay the incidental bills weekly. One week it seemed unusually large, and I said so to the woman at the desk. Her response was, "Oh, no. You should see Larry Hagman's bar bill!" Well, I thought, nice of her to tell me that.

Coincidentally, during that shoot, Gary Hart was running for president, and the League of Women Voters debate was being held in Dallas. Donna Mills asked if we'd like to come as her guests to the debate, as she was a friend of Hart's. I don't know that Ken was all that interested, but he knew I would be, as my early interest in politics never abated. We were in a small room watching the televised debate when a secret service agent found us and said Mr. Hart would like us to join him afterward for a small party in his hotel suite. And it really was a small party: Gary Hart, Donna Mills (who brought her hairdresser!), Ken and me, Penny Marshall, Warren Beatty and Jack Nicholson.

I had met Beatty before, with Julie Christie, at the Peretz's house in Cambridge during the Vietnam era. Beatty was very political and a comfortable guy in private company. He was also really smooth at making short work of women who pursued him. I once saw him charmingly tell a woman to give him a call at his apartment at the Beverly Hilton Hotel. She was thrilled to have this private information. The thing was, he actually lived at the Beverly Wilshire. (This, of course, was long before Annette Bening and his living in an actual house.)

Anyway, at Hart's little after-party, Beatty was zeroing in on me. Long stares, questions addressed to me; he kind of play-vamped me. I do not for one minute believe he was seriously interested; that's just what he did, as though it were his mission in life to always be hitting on *someone,* and the pool that night was very small. (Later, this would be said of Bill Clinton.) At some point Nicholson and I went into the kitchen to make coffee for everyone, and we talked politics. I would like to claim I don't know what this says about me (though I actually do), but if I were single that night I would have wandered off with Nicholson, not Beatty. I found him to be whip-smart, dangerous, and a major talent, making him irresistible—which is not to say that Ken Howard was anyone's idea of a consolation prize.

In 1982 we were at the very first Night of 100 Stars (theoretically the showbiz crème de la crème), which taped at Radio City Music Hall—for five hours. Ken was not sure how he made the cut, but he did, and it was something quite special. Princess Grace was there, along with major stage and screen stars. I have no idea why, but I was one of the few spouses allowed in the green room—in this case an extremely large space that more properly might have been called "the green ballroom." The producer, Alex Cohen, knowing the taping would take a long time, mandated there be no bar, thereby forestalling the possibility of dealing with a bunch of drunk actors. Of course Elizabeth Taylor was there. When I saw her sitting on a sofa with Zev Braun, a movie producer, I casually said to my husband, "Would you like to meet Elizabeth Taylor?" He was thrilled, and I brought him to the sofa. What I did not know was that she'd brought her own bar with her in a paper bag and was three sheets to the wind. I bent my knees to be somewhat at eye level with her and picked a most unfortunate opening salvo.

"I will never forget your babysitting me in Palm Springs when I was twelve."

This had, in fact, happened. We were at the Biltmore, and so was she, along with her then-beau, Stanley Donen. She and Mother became pals at the pool. She was very sweet to me and autographed thirty pictures of herself for my class. One day Mother said she and Father had a party that night and no maids were free to sit. Elizabeth said she had a script to read, so she and Stanley would look after me. And they did. I was insane with excitement. We three had dinner on the porch of our casita, and then she told me to do my homework and when I was tired to go to bed. Oh my. Her eyes really were lavender, and she had a double row of lashes.

I would see her a few more times over the years in Chicago, as Kup always entertained the movie stars when they laid over on their way to Los Angeles on the Super Chief. On these occasions, Kup's daughter, Cookie, would invite her besties over to get a look at the visiting celebrities.

Well, that night at Radio City Music Hall, Ms. Taylor did not remember Palm Springs and she did not remember me. La Taylor just sat there looking at me with raised eyebrows. Now a normal person would have felt the chill and immediately retreated. I, however, have always been afflicted with the utterly self-defeating, if not masochistic, habit of becoming nervous and continuing to talk. So I yammered on, and at no time did she say a word. When it became painful to watch, Ken took my elbow and led me away. Only then did I realize that an aging movie star might not appreciate a grown woman pointing out the age differ-ence—even if it was only eight years.

Ken walked with me over to Betty Bacall to recover. She liked him very much and therefore was quite sweet to me—not her usual mode, I was later told. I obsessed over my faux pas with Elizabeth but did manage to pull through.

Living in LA was sometimes grist for my mill. I wrote a Diarist for the *New Republic* that got me labeled an East Coast snob, which was kind of funny because I was a Midwesterner, and except for my years at Brandeis I'd spent much of my life in Chicago. I merely mentioned that "dressing up" on the left coast most often meant shoes and socks, and I quoted someone writing in the *Los Angeles Herald-Examiner* who remarked on the excesses of the Hollywood rich: "You get the feeling that God did not rest on the seventh day but created the sequin." I also pointed out that the garage at the old Getty Museum was carpeted—but I was even-handed and wrote that it was nothing Persian, merely Astroturf. And of course I couldn't resist mentioning that when I went shopping for a bookcase, the saleswoman asked if I were putting up plants.

I had heard about a group in LA called L.A.D.I.E.S., which stood for "life after divorce is eventually sane." There was actu-ally a support group for women who had been married to movie stars and needed help learning to live without perks like limos, first-class plane tickets, and other luxuries. It had been started by Patty Lewis (Mrs. Jerry) and Lynn Langdon (Mrs. Michael). Patty had been dumped, after more than thirty years and five children, for a stewardess whose named was spelled "Sandee." Lynn was dismissed when Michael wanted to marry his makeup artist.

No journalists had ever been allowed to attend any L.A.D.I.E.S. meetings or write about them, but I guess, even in my married state, I was considered a sister. My first thought, just hearing about the group, was that it must be entertaining to listen to women wailing about the loss of limousines. But the stories were really sad, and not what I expected. Many of these ex-wives were poorly if not dishonestly treated in terms of financial settlements, and one of Mickey Rooney's former wives was living in her car. A lot of these women were not trained to have a meaningful job, and sometimes their children got short shrift as well. As for the departed movie star husbands, saints these men were not. The L.A.D.I.E.S. group (some of whom did have real money) adopted another group of divorced women who had no skills, no movie-star exes, and no resources. They'd been dumped in middle-age with rather hopeless futures. The Hollywood "big sisters" organized ways for these women to become trained to earn a living on their own.

On two occasions I was able to combine my work with Ken's. In both instances I wrote pieces for *TV Guide* shilling (subtly, I thought) for his latest *oeuvres*.

My first effort to hype a show of his—Mark Twain's *Pudd'nhead Wilson* in 1984—paid off in spades. It got the highest ratings American Playhouse had ever had. I, however, got in a lot of trouble with that piece—at least in the state of West Virginia. Although I made myself a city girl cliché, feigning fear of the snakes I'd been warned about and grumbling about the bark-all-night dogs in the trailer park across the ravine, the good citizens of Harper's Ferry thought I was making fun of them. I was, of course, making fun of myself, as I thought was evident from my opening sentence: "Nobody knows the truffles I've seen." In any case, the locals flooded the *TV Guide* mailroom and their secretary of state wrote a letter to the editor saying I was no longer welcome in the state of West Virginia!

The second time I tried being a stealth publicist was when Ken made *Strange Interlude*, starring opposite Glenda Jackson, for a combined BBC/PBS production in 1988. That piece, too, was for *TV Guide*, and it turned out to be that week's cover story, with a picture of Ken and Glenda in period clothes in a small rowboat. We were in London for two glorious months, with an unheard of four weeks of rehearsal. The director, of course, was English, and everyone was stage-trained. Ken, to my amazement, was recognized all over London because of *Dynasty* and *The Colbys*. (I shouldn't have been surprised though, because *The White Shadow* had been the top-rated show in Turkey. I think people not in the business are unaware of the fact that American TV shows are sold all over the world, even if they have to be dubbed. We once watched the Spanish version of *La Sombra Blanca*, which, in today's terms, would be akin to setting your iPhone's Siri to talk to you in Chinese and just laughing.)

This trip, however, turned out to be tumultuous. We had gone to Scotland beforehand so Ken could golf at Turnberry. (Like it or not, bagpipes every day at 5:00 p.m. sharp.) I had started having severe stomach pain. When we got to London we settled into the "flat" that had been arranged for us. (It was actually Douglas Fairbanks, Jr.'s apartment in the building next to the Basil Street Hotel.) I knew I was in trouble, so I called my mother who had very good medical connections. She called her friend Fleur Cowles in London, now married to "Tom, the Timber King" who happened to sit on a medical panel by grace of the Queen Mum.

I can't speak about Britain's socialized medicine, but Harley Street docs are as good as they come. I went to see Sir Anthony Dawson, known as "the Queen's bowel doctor." I was quite surprised to learn the Queen *had* bowels, but it did give me confidence in Sir Anthony. I liked him very much, though it turned out my difficulty was not in his field, but was, rather, a female problem. I'd had a partial hysterectomy when I was 45, and the Boston surgeon did me the favor of leaving me one ovary. That's where the trouble was. Two years later, now 1988, it was not possible to determine malignancy in any other way than exploratory surgery, so three days after I'd met Dr. Dawson I was being operated on by "Mr." Shepherd, the English designation for a surgeon. I had great confidence in him. He was very straight about what might go on in the operating theater, should cancer be present, and he had also been Dr. Dawson's first choice for an oncologic gynecological surgeon.

My mother was beside herself with anxiety but she'd been advised not to fly over lest it would lead me to think I might be dying. Ken was a wreck, as well, and did, in fact, send for Cricket, who checked out of Vassar for a week to be with us. I realized from that experience that the person who is potentially very sick—at the center of the drama, if you will—may be the person in the best emotional shape of everyone involved. Perhaps it was my gambler's instinct and the gift of acceptance that helped me understand that "it's gonna be what it's gonna be."

The night before surgery Ken, Cricket and I had a wonderful dinner, at which he gave me a beautiful pair of tourmaline and gold earrings from Tiffany's. I named them the "Please Don't Die" earrings because I think that was the message of the gift: it was tangible, and it was something meant for the future. Fortunately, I did not have cancer, but rather an endometriotic ovary, which was removed.

With Ken working all day, the executive housekeeper at the Basil Street Hotel next door looked in on me after Cricket returned to the States, at which time my mother wandered over. Once I was able to be up and about, my "grocery store" was the Food Halls of Harrods, an experience not to be missed. "Horrids," as some locals called it, carried everything you can put in your mouth. There were furry rabbits on ice, whole baby pigs, gorgeous whole fish, massive pyramids of fruits and vegetables, seemingly miles of chocolates and sweets, more cheeses than you've ever heard of and, of course, a major wine selection. I can't imagine any American not being overwhelmed by the variety, abundance and sheer gorgeousness of "The Hall."

Ken's avocation was golf, and though he had a high handicap, he loved playing. When we joined Riviera he became one of the "fourth hole boys." The others were Dean Martin and David Wayne—like Ken, an actor who had started out on Broadway. It was Wayne, in fact, who won the first Tony Award for Best Supporting Actor, the same one Ken would win years later. When it was still the LA Open (before a corporate name was attached), it was always held at Riviera. There was a powerful telescope in our living room, and Ken called from the studio one day during the Open to have me look and tell him who was on the fourth hole. As familiar with golf as I was with hockey, I did the only sensible thing and read the names on the golf bags to identify the players. I duly reported that the twosome on hole four was Mr. Ping and Mr. Wilson.

The celebrity pro-ams, which Ken loved, were perhaps what impeded his game. All the famous pros were giving him advice, but the advice was not always the same. My favorite event was the Crosby in Pebble Beach, before it morphed into the AT & T Pebble Beach National Pro-Am. Nathanial Crosby had met Ken at Riviera and invited him. The celebrities and corporate executives at the Crosby were an unpredictable and eclectic mix because they were invited by members of the Crosby family rather than being offered up by PR firms. We went for a number of years.

It was at the Crosby that we would see Louise and Alan Shepard. Although we were once-a-year friends, I always enjoyed seeing them. Given that he was the first American astronaut in space, there was a lack of grandiosity to him, and he had no desire to put himself forward in a social setting. On more than one occasion, there was a knowing look between us when some jerk would try to impress him. But it was always worse when the person didn't know who Shepard was.

My favorite episode was at cocktails one night before dinner. I was in a small conversational group with Shepard when a blowhard joined us and found a way to announce that he had flown in on his own jet, and he always asked one of his pilots to vacate the seat so he could fly the plane himself. Having *no* idea who Shepard was, he addressed him and asked, "Do you fly?" That adorable man said, "Why yes. Yes I do." And he went no further, sparing the jerk great embarrassment.

It is a tricky proposition to recognize when, exactly, a relationship starts to go off the rails. It may, in fact, be unknowable—unless, of course, it's an undeniable and clear-cut event, such as an abusive situation where a woman calls the cops, saying through a fat lip that her husband just coldcocked her. In other words, I don't really know when trouble found us, but my best recollection is that it was on one side or the other of our being together for ten years. Ken and I shared a strong bond, and in some ways he was dependent on me. There was, however, one issue that we ultimately could not settle, and with time it grew more fractious. Our single, fundamental disagreement was just that: a disagreement. I felt he had a problem with alcohol. He disagreed.

My concerns escalated when different Kens started to show up with greater frequency, personalities that, before then, had made only brief appearances. He was angrier more often. His expressions of sentimentality or amorousness came with a syrupy insistence; they didn't feel like real conversation. The declarations were schmaltzy and awkward for me, as though some man in a bar had got hold of me and wouldn't stop talking. All these deviations were unleashed, of course, after he'd been drinking. In the early days I objectively saw that he was a big drinker, but it hadn't, then, altered his behavior. As he pointed out to me, when you're six foot six, your capacity for alcohol is quite large. And as I realized later, alcoholism is progressive.

With a history of somatizing, my long-ago stomach trouble (of the spastic colon variety) returned. The hovering threat of my having to deal with his not-sober self was literally making me sick. The elephant in our room had a lampshade on its head. I could not square the Ken Howard I had known for years with the Ken Howard who put his fist through a wall, started throwing every piece of crockery he could get his hands on in the kitchen at the farm, and stripped the linens off our bed—with me in it—at two in the morning. Nor with the man who stuffed his pocket with a fistful of cold shrimp at a Pebble Beach cocktail party, not to be discovered until the closet started smelling like Fisherman's Wharf.

There was, unfortunately, a family history of alcoholism. At the extreme end was his much younger brother, Donnie, who died in his late forties of cirrhosis of the liver. In addition to family issues, I always thought ambivalence about the entertainment industry caused him to self-medicate. Many years later, I read in *The Richard Burton Diaries* a passage that seemed to sum up what I think Ken must have been struggling with as well:

> *I am fundamentally so bored with my job that only drink is capable of killing the pain.... All my life I think I have been secretly ashamed of being an actor and the older I get the more ashamed I get. Why keep doing it? I like being famous and money is very important...*

My guess is that Ken's ambivalence about his career was not as deeply rooted as Burton's, but it was there. To my knowledge, the only time during our fourteen years together that he spoke publicly about his conflicted feelings concerning acting was in a 1977 interview with Cleveland Amory when he said, "I do know that if you are big they're convinced you're not talented, and they're utterly convinced you've got to be stupid. Honestly, I've been in meetings where they explain everything in words of one syllable.... Actually, if you're a blond WASP these days they're also utterly convinced you... couldn't have any real emotion." He was too modest to say "big—and handsome," but that was definitely part of the equation.

In a slow-moving metamorphosis, he just seemed no longer comfortable in his own skin. I am fairly certain Ken knew he had a problem because when I suggested that he just *try* AA, he said he might if he weren't so famous. This demur had to be an excuse born of denial. There were big, big stars who had cleaned up from both alcohol *and* drugs who were doing just fine. In fact, it often proved to be a good career move, being a dog whistle to Hollywood that the substance abuse problems of yesteryear were no more. In 1985 I started getting love notes, apologizing for boozy behavior the night before. Always warm and loving, using pet names for me, he reiterated his love for me and blamed the regrettable conduct on demons, moodiness and frustration... as well as noting that his sobriety would be good for both of us.

Those notes said many things. One, he knew alcohol was doing him no favors. Two, we really did love each other. And three, we kept trying. In 1985 he was doing both *Dynasty* and *The Colbys*. This was, for him, like being trapped in a gold mine. He was being paid *a lot* of money for being in both those prime-time hits. The weekly checks were for tens of thousands of dollars, but the shows were dreck, and he knew it. So did Aaron Spelling, who correctly predicted that his haute couture soaps would finally become onerous for Ken, given his stage and high-end television history. Because they had the same agent at CAA, Spelling said although the contract was for three years, if, after a year, Ken felt the need to leave, he could. No harm, no foul.

In addition to the heavy-breathing story lines, the only people who worked a full five-day week were "the girls" (Joan Collins and Linda Evans) and John Forsythe. I called it "a dead movie star show" because actors like Ric Montalban, Rock Hudson, Barbara Stanwyck, and George Hamilton had been working only one day a week. Though no "dead movie star," Ken often had that same one-day-a-week schedule, maybe two, giving him a lot of time to play golf and wind up at the Riviera bar (where he saw a lot of Dean Martin).

What he did—quitting after one year—was almost unheard of because few actors (voluntarily) leave a lucrative, popular prime-time show—let alone two of them. It was a long shot, but he called Bob Brustein, the founder and artistic director of the American Repertory Theater at Harvard. Brustein had been Ken's dean at Yale Drama School. His request? To join the rep company for a year to clear his head. Brustein said no one well known had ever done that, but he would figure something out, and yes, by all means, come.

As a Harvard *Crimson* headline put it: "Ken Howard: Leaving Hollywood for Harvard." The story quoted him as saying he found *Dynasty* "unstimulating" and that "Nobody works that hard, and the material is sort of a hoot…I was more interested in golf and book reading than in what I was doing." So in 1987 we were off to Cambridge and our Harvard year. He would work with avante garde directors such as Andrei Serban, Robert Wilson, Julie Taymor and Richard Foreman.

With his spot in the repertory company came a teaching slot at Harvard, so he crafted the first rhetoric course the college had offered in fifty years. Of course the kids were lined up knee-deep to get into the class because, to them, he was "The White Shadow." The number of applicants was such that Ken decided there would have to be auditions. The kids knocked themselves out with long, prepared statements about why they should be accepted into the class. I remember one young man did a wonderful bit purposely confusing Ken with Ron Howard, going on and on about having loved him from when he first saw him playing Opie. (That kid made the cut.) Ken even added an extra section—and still there wasn't room for everyone who wanted to take the class. He also created a class at Harvard Law School with our friend, Charlie Nesson, the Weld Professor of Law, wherein the students were taught presentational and oratorical skills for future litigators. Even a few noted professors, such as Charles Ogletree, took the course.

We also went to Paris with the company for a three-week run of Julie Taymor's *King Stag*, which played in the suburb of Bobigny. Ken wanted to live over there as the rest of the company did, in a small Left Bank hotel, which we did check into, but the room could not have housed the luggage and us, so we were outta there. We were both such brats by this time that we moved to the Plaza Athénée for three weeks—the only hotel each of us had ever stayed in over there. The thing about Hollywood's bloated salaries, for those lucky enough to get them, is that you're pretty much enabled to do whatever you want. And on top of that, you never see the bills because movie people pulling down serious money have theatrical financial offices that pay them.

Cambridge was certainly tonic after Los Angeles. It had deciduous trees! And seasons! Ken loved what he was doing and looked forward to getting up in the morning and not winding up in a makeup chair. We had a very jazzy social life, mostly thanks to my old friends Marty and Anne Peretz, whose dinner parties were as close to a salon as you can get. We loved Cambridge and I suggested to Ken he might want to consider changing his life, both because he was conflicted about "the business," and his career had slowed. I thought Amherst, his alma mater, or maybe even Harvard, would be thrilled to have him in their drama department. He told me he couldn't make a change like that because, he said, "I'm an actor." However, we both liked Cambridge so much that we bought an apartment there during his year at the American Repertory Theater. Having sold his place in New York, Cambridge seemed like the perfect East Coast *pied-à-terre*. While I felt Ken was happier, I guess he wasn't happy enough, because people were always telling me that they saw him at the bar at the Harvest, an upscale restaurant halfway between the theater and our apartment. When the Harvard year ended, we returned to Los Angeles.

In the early years of our marriage, following his professional success, it was often said that Ken Howard would age into being the next Henry Fonda. Like Fonda, his persona was that of a handsome, classy male lead. But for whatever reason, when we returned to LA the bloom was off the rose in terms of the roles he was being offered.

As is standard operating procedure in Hollywood, at least for those who came from the stage, Ken accepted an offer to go *back* to the stage. Such a move can be a career-rejuvenating fresh start, something like a ship's repositioning cruise.

He was cast in Neil Simon's *Rumors* in September of 1988. We camped out in San Diego for six weeks while the play was being worked out at the Old Globe Theatre in its pre-Broadway tryout. Simon, called "Doc" because he was a great play doctor, had a particular way of tuning up his *own* new work. He would sit in the audience during rehearsals and rewrite as he saw the characters interact. The play, about four affluent couples and, well, rumors, starred Ken, Christine Baranski, Andre Gregory, Ron Leibman, Jessica Walter, Joyce Van Patten, and relative newcomers Lisa Banes and Mark Nelson.

Ken had worked for Simon before and was told he would be first among equals. The weak sister here, alas, was Banes, who was unfortunately playing opposite Ken. The marvelous Christine Baranski was paired with Nelson. As Doc Simon watched the rehearsals, he shrunk the roles of Ken and Banes. Ken felt double-crossed when Simon started to write away from him, thereby diminishing his role, so he instructed his theater agent, Lionel Larner, to read the contract carefully and find an out so he could leave the Broadway run as soon as legally permissible. The play moved to New York and opened at the Broadhurst in mid-November of 1988. It was a matter of weeks before Ken left the show. Well, *nobody* walks out of a Neil Simon show on Broadway, and Simon was furious. While I thought it was wildly unfair—and worse, I knew it to be untrue—the stage manager breezed it around, to save face, that Ken was "let go" because of his drinking. The problem was that, although the rumor, no pun intended, was false, it was credible to some because Ken was known to be a drinker, which is why the stage manager said it in the first place. The disappointment of *Rumors* did not do our marriage any good.

I knew, deep down, we weren't going to make it. We would spend time apart, and then come together. Repeat and rinse. On

November 7, 1990, I wrote him a letter that pretty much tells the whole story:

> *You have promised, tried, and failed to stop drinking*
> *on your own. The problem with your backsliding is*
> *that, when drunk, you invariably tell me, "Let me go.*
> *I want a divorce, my life is better in your absence."*
> *This has become too painful and punishing and is*
> *no longer acceptable to me.*
>
> *I give you back your "list" of complaints not to*
> *be a petty historian of our troubles, but to let you*
> *know . . . what I've been hearing for a very long time.*
> *You attack me for my wit, my use of language, my*
> *affinity for the news, phonies, lesser values, and*
> *my harshness . . . And during this last disastrous*
> *and destructive THREE-HOUR call from Paris,*
> *you announced you would dance on my grave.*
> *Surely this kind of talk is in the same category*
> *as putting the handful of shrimp in your pocket*
> *at Pebble Beach and starting to pee on the carpet*
> *in numerous hotels . . .*
>
> *You have repeatedly said "I will give up nothing*
> *for this relationship." I think you're talking about*
> *alcohol . . . Surely an activity that alters your*
> *behavior, makes you fat, and destroys a love and*
> *friendship of many years can have nothing to*
> *recommend hanging on to it . . . I will no longer*
> *listen to your saying—sometimes on alternate*

days — that I am the truest, most supportive friend
you have, AND that I am cold and harsh and now
that the kids are grown there is no reason to be
together. If you cannot achieve resolution about
what it is you think, and want, and are willing
to do, I can at least take myself out of your
drama. We need a new beginning or we need
an end.

This situation for me was the equivalent of knowing the words but not the music. In my starter marriage I experienced, firsthand, the trouble that alcohol abuse can cause. I also knew of my mother's belief that booze was the major factor in many marriages falling apart — her own included. I was aware, certainly, that this formerly marvelous union was on life support, but it took me more than three years to finally make up my mind to call it a day. I think the indecision (unusual for me) stemmed from the fact that I had hope and certainly the wish that we could get back what we had.

I began to read AA literature. Two of their tenets proved to be determinative for me. One, you could not *make* anyone want to get well. And two, a person has an alcohol problem if someone close to them thinks they do. In a move that was odd, at least for me, I bought Melody Beattie's book, *Codependent No More*. Never inclined toward how-to or self-help books, a friend put me onto this one, which I did read — and bingo. I made my decision. We would separate and divorce.

In 1991, I had to decide where I would live — on my own. I had the whole country to choose from, having no reason to be in one city as opposed to another. My children were grown and scattered between two continents (Adam loved Europe), and my career was portable. I eliminated Chicago and New York, but I knew I wanted an antidote to Hollywood.

Of course that antidote was Cambridge, land of the smart people, no glitz, and seriously devoted to understatement. Ken figured out I would land there before I'd even made the decision. The absence of fancy cars, boob jobs, face-lifts, agents, managers and personal trainers was most appealing. (In the Palisades we actually had Jake, himself, as in "Body by Jake.") Cambridge was also a comfortable place for old babes on the loose. Single women could go anywhere they wished—unescorted—even black-tie events. My guess is that the heavy concentration of academics and writers is why Cambridge was this way. Couples often had different jobs and obligations and couldn't—or didn't feel the need to—always be seen together. Cambridge was about what you had to say, not who was on your arm. Women (whether widowed, divorced or lesbian) stood alone relative to their accomplishment, ergo they could stand alone socially, as well. Another allure of Cambridge was that I had good friends there. And an apartment.

Several weeks after we were living apart and officially separated, Ken came to Cambridge to see me. We had a loving, warm chat. He surprisingly told me a few deep secrets that had nothing to do with me (which surprised me, but I suppose this was indicative of longtime habits being hard to break). And we talked about his plans. At that point, his career was pretty much going nowhere.

After that visit he would call periodically from Los Angeles just to talk. I asked, more than once, if he had started dating, because I had.

"No," he said. "I still feel married."

"That is nuts," I told him. "Please find yourself some interesting female company."

Then one night I got a call from him. He was in the manager's office of an Italian restaurant we liked.

"I'm on a date! I am with two stuntwomen," he said, laughing.

"Perfect!" I said, then immediately wished I hadn't, because my response sounded as if he'd said he was with two strippers, or two pole dancers...and what if one of them became his new flame?

After a year's separation, I told him I would see to the divorce details because I was on the East Coast, where the divorce would be granted. Our financial office (the one that prepared the income tax returns, paid SAG dues and paid all the bills) decided it should take place in Connecticut, where we owned property. We worked out the agreement ourselves because the division just seemed obvious—and there was no rancor, just sadness. I gave up any rights to his pension plan (save for a token sum I had to take, by law), all his residuals, including the very lucrative work he'd done during our marriage, and we split a large cash and investment account. We each wanted to be generous to honor the underlying affection. I remember offering him a Ken Noland painting he'd picked out and he declined, saying he wanted to leave the apartment just as it was.

I got the Cambridge condo because he could not live on the East Coast. He would've gotten the farm—except for the fact that it no longer belonged to me. At some point during the mid-1980s, my mother's financial people told her to start moving money out of her estate for tax purposes. She made some handsome gifts to me and the children, and one way to transfer a lot of money to me was to buy the farm for its appraised value, then $1.4 million, with the understanding that, at her death, she would deed it back to me, which in effect would have been to us. Alas, the divorce meant there would be no "us," so she gave the property to Harvard, knowing I would not use the house alone. It had, after all, been a place for Ken to recharge when he wasn't working.

We were sending paperwork back and forth, and one morning a FedEx envelope came with his signature on the divorce agreement. He included a note with many endearments. Later in the day I played a message he'd left on my machine. He said when he signed everything he'd been almost dysfunctional, but the next morning was better—and I would be fine, too, on the morrow.

My plan was to go to Connecticut with a car and driver, but a girlfriend, Ann Lambert, said I would do no such thing. She was coming with me, saying that such an undertaking is nothing one does alone. Ann was really the perfect buddy for that day because we'd named ourselves "The Ex-Wives of Amherst Club." And an exclusive group we were: just the two of us, Ann having divorced a classmate of Ken's. She rented a car and we were off to picture-book Litchfield. She reminisced about when we had first met, ten years earlier at a dinner Ken gave for his Amherst chums in Boston. What she remembered was so lovely that I wrote it in a note to my mother: "The light of your feeling for each other fairly bounced off the walls," and she found our relationship to be "shimmering." When we got back to Cambridge there was a massive bouquet on my dining room table. The card said, "With thanks and much love, Babar." (That being just one of the pet names I called him. Probably the name he used most for me was "Softy," because of my skin.)

The next day I sent him a mini-report of the trip to Litchfield, telling him "The Ex-Wives of Amherst Club" had a great drive…

losing only twenty minutes because Ann, for no reason other than Freudian, took the Amherst exit. The courthouse was a charming New England stone building, and in the judge's chambers was her gorgeous, big Bernese Mountain Dog. It had been a short, easy, pro forma procedure. Just a couple of questions, a signature, *et voila*. The odd thing to me was how transforming the day was. Although I'd felt divorced for the past year, there was something magical about the day. It may have to do with something he'd pointed out to me years ago: formal closures and symbols are powerful. And I mentioned my utter surprise to return home to find his simply beautiful flowers. For me, they commemorated the best failed marriage there ever was. And I ended my "report" by telling him: "You know what? It's still true: we beat 'em. Over and out."

If our marriage had been accompanied by music, I think the songs would have been, in order: "Just in Time," "Those Were the Days, My Friend," "What'll I Do?" and "It Was Just One of Those Things." The divorce was finalized on February 5, 1992. The formalities, however, did not necessarily signal Howard's end. I had great residual fondness for him, as he did for me. I also owed this lovely guy a great debt. He'd been a wonderful father to my two younger children and had brought Cricket and me closer together. And oh, the fun and good times we'd had. If one had to leave, it felt good to leave a marriage this way.

He did end up marrying one of the stuntwomen—"the stuntress," as his pal Joe Allen called her—on February 12, a week after our divorce was final. And to my surprise, on Valentine's Day, just days after he remarried, he wrote me a letter letting me know that all was well, he was happy and he missed me. This struck me as a little odd, but sweet.

The next "Hi, Softy" note I got was dated July 28 of that year, telling me what a good visit he'd had with Adam, who was now making movies, and that he talked with Cricket on the phone, and how happy it made him to connect with the kids.

The last written communication I got from him was in April of 1993, following a phone call. He was going to check on Adam and Cricket and said it was good to hear my voice, my words. And he used a funny sign-off, next to a drawn heart: GLATFW. That was the code in my mother's office for responding to readers who were just nattering on about nothing in particular. It stood for "Good luck and thanks for writing." Enclosed was a picture of him taking a swing at Pebble Beach in 1993. He'd written on it, "Another missed putt! Bring back memories, Softy?"

And then nothing until 1997, when Cricket was accepted to medical school. He called and said, "We did it, didn't we?"

Ken's career moved to doing guest shots, a few plays, smaller parts in movies, and a series here and there that didn't get much attention. In 2009 he became president of the Screen Actors Guild. From the time we had parted, I very much wanted to see his career resurrected, and because I still had friends in the business, mine was the hidden hand suggesting, now and then, that he would be wonderful in (fill in the blank).

One such effort, which happened in 1997 or 1998, had a surprising outcome. Fran Weissler was a friend of mine who produced Broadway revivals with her husband, Barry. (I saw opening nights of *Chicago* in three different cities!) When it was clear that the *Chicago* revival was a smash, I asked Fran if she didn't agree that Ken would be perfect for the lawyer role played by Jimmy

Naughton (who had also been a Williamstowner). She said that was, indeed, a good idea and they would make him an offer for one of the touring companies. I was astonished when she got back to me and said he'd turned it down. Apparently he didn't wish to do the proverbial "eight a week."

In the summer of 2008 the artistic director of the New Repertory Theatre in Watertown (near Boston) called to tell me that Ken would be doing a show for them, and she wanted me to hear it from her before I read about it. I said that was wonderful and of course I would be there. It was *According to Tip*, a one-man show about Boston's native son, Tip O'Neill.

I decided to have a dinner party before the show with Charlie and Fern Nesson, friends from our Harvard year, and Cricket and Spike, her future husband, who would come from New York to join us. I told everyone it would be a surprise; we would go to dinner, see the show, and then go backstage afterward to surprise him. Cricket, perhaps wisely, did not think it should be a surprise, so she told Ken of our plans. He instructed her, quite adamantly, to convey the message that I should not come backstage. At dinner, we tossed this new development around and figured this wasn't really coming from him but probably his wife. It has been said that new wives don't like old history. I'm guessing I was troublesome for her, or at least the idea of me was. After some conversation about this at dinner, we decided we would try anyway. When the curtain came down, we did—and the stage manager cut us off at the pass. No one was allowed backstage, she said. I was kind of surprised, and of course sad that my friendly divorce was no longer so friendly.

CHAPTER SEVEN

Wherein I was between husbands,
while he was between cupcakes.

What would be the dumbest thing that a newly separated fifty-one-year-old woman could do just nine days after she arrives in a new town to make a new life? I think it would be to call an old bad-boy boyfriend. And that is exactly what I did.

Dallying with a married man seldom ends well. (For you, that is. He is usually fine.) For a period of time it is fun, dangerous and exciting—as secrets often are. Except that it's often not a secret, and the time will come when you'll think: just shoot me. Or better yet, shoot *him*.

This is not an attempt to defend what is less-than-honorable behavior, but grown-up girls having a bad-boy boyfriend is more common than people might think. And the secret handshake for this band of women is the code word "complicated." Whenever a woman says she is in a "complicated relationship," that almost always means he's married.

I would not recommend going the borrowed husband route, but I will admit it was interesting. And instructive.

My borrowed husband (B.H.) had many things going for him. One was a lot of experience in being borrowed. By the time I got to him he'd already had dalliances too numerous to add up. It would not surprise me if there were spreadsheets somewhere in a locked desk drawer.

He did not stumble into affairs. They were a choice he made long ago: in the third year of his decades-long marriage, to be precise. Did he ever care for someone enough to leave his marriage? Apparently not, though he said he'd once considered it but decided he couldn't see himself living with the woman's young child. This made sense to me because I'd found him emotionally stingy.

When I asked how many times he'd been in love, he thought for what seemed like a long time and then answered, "One and a half." One and a *half*? I actually found myself hoping that it was his wife who'd received the whole vote. I did not know who the half might have been. It might have been me for all I knew.

B.H. was a great one for discretion. I was not. I also think he was ambivalent about being discreet because we did surprisingly public things, like opening nights and "business dinners" at the best restaurants. I sometimes put a notebook on the table so if push came to shove, he could say he was being interviewed.

His stated wish, nonetheless, was that our relationship be kept quiet. That was not my wish, and I told pretty much everyone. As a friend explained to me later, I just wasn't the type to live in anyone's closet.

I do think B.H. had his girlfriend routine down to a science. Only by happenstance did I figure out that perhaps it was customary for him to send two dozen roses the morning after — well, the morning after the relationship had crossed the line into illicit. Confirmation that this was a tradition with him came when the florist he used (in my neighborhood) mentioned, the next time he saw me, that B.H. was a nice guy who had sent exactly the same lavish bouquet some months earlier to a woman he then named.

This information caused me to think for a minute: were florists bound by the same confidentiality rules as priests, shrinks and lawyers? They were not. After evaluating what I knew of the recipient's business relationship to B.H., I thought, *Right. This is his* M.O., and I tucked the information away. With his history he very well could have a standing order.

We are talking Major Player here. In any case, after the inaugural bouquet, flowers started coming from a florist near his office, paid for in cash. I learned that anything having to do with me was paid for in cash. When we traveled, for instance, he would hand over his office-arranged ticket, then pay for mine in cash. And I was instructed never to answer a telephone in a hotel room.

Something else I figured out that was probably formulaic was that the first gift for a special occasion would be a gold-and-diamond bauble. From then on the presents were clothes. But he did pick them out himself, probably not trusting his secretary enough to delegate this job.

Speaking of whom, to keep her out of his private life as much as possible, he had on his desk a private line that I named the "bimbo phone." Except there were times when I did go through his secretary, and she never asked why I was calling. Hmmm.

All of us "other women" find ways to tell ourselves that we are different from the *other* other women; that we are special. The way I found to do this was somewhat unusual.

When our affair was relatively new, a friend of mine was hired to work in B.H.'s office. When she told me of her employment, I had to clue her in about, uh, developments, and we decided it would be mutually beneficial if we did not let on that we knew each other. This made for a wonderful two-way flow of information between us. About him. Furthermore, because he often talked business with me, I had quite a bit of information.

And that's the way I came to feel special: when my friend realized she would need a new job. I told her, about a year into her tenure, that I had basically kept her employed through pillow talk for some months, but the ax was soon to fall.

Without saying I knew her, I told B.H., whenever he complained about her work, that I'd heard her life was at sixes and sevens; therefore, he could not fire her, at least for a while. He simply had to be responsive to the Hebrew concept of *rachmones* (which means compassion).

She confided to two senior men in the office that she knew she was going to be let go, and could they help her find a new position? Well, they wondered, how did she know this? She explained that her good friend was the boss's close friend. They could hardly believe it.

They had a million questions, foremost among them: Was the friend close to her in age?

"Older," she told them.

They were stunned, it being totally out of character for him to have a girlfriend who was fifty-something. The boss's babes were usually young and of the nurse/flight-attendant variety.

"But this woman is ten years younger than he is," my friend said.

The men said that hardly counted, seeing as how it approached age-appropriate. When my friend described me and my life, she said the two men were positively thrilled. How wonderful, they said, that B.H. would finally have some emotional support from a grown-up.

And that is how I came to feel special. I was not his type. His associates even found the relationship salutary. (If you are getting the idea that pretty much everyone knew he ran around, you are right on the money.)

You should know that B.H., on the surface, was not an obvious choice. He was wiry and not particularly good looking, certainly no hunk like the actor to whom I had been formerly married. Continuing down the debit column, he often had the same chilliness I despised in my starter husband. He was simply unavailable, in every sense of the word.

What he had that I found interesting were intellect and animal magnetism. It was also hard to resist a man who tells you that he has lusted after you since meeting briefly many years earlier. I was the girl in his head, which is probably why he was able to deviate from his pattern of cupcakes. He also made it seem as though he really liked women, in that way that narcissists do. And he was supremely confident, always an appealing trait in a man. He told me, "Once I'm with a woman and it's good, I own her forever." We shared an interest in politics, the same kind of humor, and we knew some of the same people. Of course we also shared what any woman and a married man share: limited time together.

He even had a philosophy about all this. I mean he actually had rules for philandering, not to mention rationales. One policy was that Saturday nights he returned to "home port," as he put it. That way there was an out, should he be seeing more than one, um, friend, who wanted to be with him on a Saturday night.

He said this didn't apply to me, of course. Of course. I had by then decided that his wife was either very understanding, occupied with other things or, by this time, essentially sick to death of him.

Interestingly, two men for whose smarts I had high regard both wanted me out of this arrangement. One of them I was paying to listen to me for fifty minutes a few times a week, and the other was my son. Their take seemed somewhat mystical to me: that although I was looking for a suitable Mr. Right #4, I would not be able to even recognize him as long as I was entangled with B.H.

While I was trying to figure that one out, I did learn something else. The dear boy was cheating on me. How was such a thing possible? Who cheats on a girlfriend? Did not a wife and a mistress take up enough time in the life of a high-powered, successful man? Did he somehow have more hours in his day than other people?

Then I understood. I had become the wife.

As is probably the case with ninety-nine out of one hundred women who dally with married men, I decided it had to stop. Alas, these endings never seem to be easily accomplished. (Hence the shrink.) When I was absolutely certain the playing field was getting crowded, that gave me the impetus to dismiss him. I scheduled a Saturday lunch, nothing particularly unusual for us, and gave him the news along with the dessert.

I will say this: He had a remarkable array of reasons why I should reconsider and keep him in my life. And he did this ad hoc, no less. Unless, of course, he had had to do it before.

I remember that walking back to my place after lunch, he asked me if he could come up, just one last time. I found myself answering with a line my mother had used in another context: "Sorry, but the last time was the last time."

I guess the lesson here, beyond the obvious, is not to have an affair with a writer.

CHAPTER EIGHT

Wherein I discover love among the ruins.

My, time flies when you're sabotaging yourself. After six years with B.H. I was finally able to unwind from this self-inflicted *folie à deux*. I was also by then fifty-seven years old, not exactly prime time for single women. I had no idea if I would marry again, but I did know I wasn't ready to hang up my peignoir...calamities here and there notwithstanding. I had been part of a couple from the time I'd been in high school, and it was my preferred way of life. Although I accepted dates with different people during B.H.'s tenure, I was really just going through the motions. But better late than never, my head was finally clear. And my head was also now red, as I decided that as a blonde I might've been having too much fun.

An older couple in Brookline, Ruth and Eliot Snyder, were friends of my parents from YPO and I had known them from the time I was in my teens. They had been wonderful to me when I moved to Cambridge alone, extending kindnesses like inviting me to holiday dinners. One day Ruth phoned and asked if she could give my number to a man she thought highly of. Eliot was chairman of the Beth Israel Hospital Board of Trustees, and she had just learned that Ron Weintraub, their chief of cardiothoracic surgery, was divorced. Fine by me. If I can frame this in twelve-step terms, I was five months' sober at the time.

Not quite a week later the doctor did call—for which he got points. A lot of middle-aged men are given someone's number, they put it in a suit pocket, send the suit to the cleaners and discover it—or not—six months later. The blind date doctor invited me to a jazz concert, but the date conflicted with a trip I was taking to Chicago to see Mother. We made another date for the day after I returned. It would be for after-dinner coffee or a drink because it was on a day he would be operating. He phoned that morning to say he'd be doing a second case and would stay in touch about what time he'd pick me up. At eight o'clock a nurse in the operating room with him called to say that Dr. Weintraub was doing a difficult case and would likely be delayed. At 9:30 p.m., she phoned again to say they had hit a snag and the doctor wondered if I stayed up late because he would like to call me. I said that would be fine.

Close to 10:30 p.m. he phoned. My God, he had a beautiful voice. And I remember the conversation, if only because when we hung up I thought I could not have sounded more moronic. I asked how he was, since by my reckoning he had been on his feet for several hours. He said the real question was how was the patient, and he was pleased to report the patient was doing well. I knew he had missed dinner so I asked if someone fed him while he operated. He said, uh, no…surgeons were trained to ignore the desire for food. Then I asked if he could do some parts of the surgery sitting down, since these things seemed to go on for hours. He said, uh, no, the surgeon, his resident, and the nurses all stood—just like on TV. (In my own defense, let me say I had never been in an operating room when I was awake.) We then made a dinner date for the following week on a day he knew his calendar was clear.

When he collected me at my apartment, I opened the door and saw a man who was so not my type. He resembled the actor-comedian, Alan King: balding, and avuncular. But onward. We went to an Italian restaurant in the neighborhood and sat opposite each other in a small booth. It is odd, but understood, that when middle-aged people go out for the first time their initial conversation could be titled: "And what did *you* major in?" Per the usual procedure, we exchanged information about schools attended, careers, children, grandchildren, previous marriages, parents living or dead, relatives in asylums and so on. It is a different game entirely from when we were all young and unencumbered.

Well, the doctor was most interesting, and to my great surprise, he, too, had been married three times. This certainly went a long way to making my own three divorces seem like less of an eye-popping statistic. However, his situation was more decorous than mine and certainly more poignant. Going into his last year at Harvard Medical School he had married a girl from Bryn Mawr he was crazy about. Two years later, during his surgical residency training, she died of melanoma—as he knew she would. His father, also a physician and surgeon, spotted a melanoma on her back when she was wearing a sundress. He told Ron he didn't think she was going to make it and perhaps they could have a long engagement. Ron said no. He had asked her to marry him, she enthusiastically said yes, and that's what they would do.

His father's prognosis proved correct, and two years later Ron was a twenty-six-year-old widowed surgical resident. Three years later, at age twenty-nine, he married an OR nurse with whom he went on to have two sons. That proved to be an unsuitable marriage, and after twenty-two years he asked for a divorce. Subsequent to that he married a medical device saleswoman for what turned out to be a shorter marriage of six years. (I am trying really hard not to get into the subject of women wanting to marry rich surgeons.)

As one of his stepsisters suggested to me later, her feeling was that, at an unconscious level, he'd simply given up, feeling his great love had been taken from him, thereby letting himself be chosen instead of being the one to choose. After a real heartbreak and two costly divorces, he decided he was done. For the men (and a few women) in his generation of cardiac surgeons, techniques and results had become more standardized and predictable, so he was extremely busy. He dated during his time on the loose but never with an eye to making anything permanent.

I found him erudite and out of the ordinary. He was reserved, with interests that went beyond medicine. He had majored in history at Harvard College and continued to read widely. He loved music, was athletic, and the most learned man I'd ever gone out with. After a dinner at which we lingered, he walked me home and we made another date. I was very much looking forward to seeing him again and getting to know him better. This surprised me because, well, he wasn't my type.

As was my habit, I phoned my Chicago pal Ilana to report on the date. I said I had finally met someone interesting, and as I was telling her his history I realized that she, too, had gone to Bryn Mawr. I mentioned the moving story of his first wife, and she asked if I knew her name.

I said, "Yes. It was Sondra."

I could hear Ilana taking a breath. "She was in my class, and I met your doctor. I even remember the engagement ring."

Married to a doc, herself, she said they were the very best people!

Our second date was dinner at the Harvard Club, followed by a Boston Symphony Orchestra concert. He was one of those Bostonians with inherited symphony seats. This was quite far from the way I grew up. My background was totally uncultured. Neither parent had an interest in art, and music appreciation began and ended with Pearl Bailey and Tommy Dorsey records.

At dinner before the concert, another guest in the dining room came over and kissed me hello. I started to make introductions and both men laughed. The man who'd come over to greet me was Dan Tosteson, dean of Harvard Medical School—and Ron's titular boss. It was quite mysterious to him that I knew this man at all, and with time he decided I "knew everybody"—clearly a statistical impossibility.

Our next date was for the opera. (Good grief, could a ballet be far behind?) It would be accurate to say that opera is my least favorite kind of music. The stories are usually goofy, and very often the star is mortally wounded but somehow manages to sing about it for forty minutes. This opera was *Lucia*, and Ron said it was one of his favorites. I could tell from the English translation scrolling like a stock ticker, stage left, that Lucia's brother would not let her marry the man she loved but made her marry, instead, someone who was useful to him. Or something. In the scene after the wedding we see Lucia stagger on stage from the marriage bed clutching a dagger, with blood all over her white nightgown. I whispered to Ron, "Some girls just don't like sex." He laughed, which was a good sign, because he took opera seriously. When the evening ended he deposited me at my door, apologizing for not being able to come in and visit but he had an early case the next morning. Then he kissed me on the forehead. "You missed!" I said. He laughed and walked down the hall.

I found his being in no hurry to take things to the next level quite interesting…and unusual. I knew he wasn't gay, and from my observations he was too mature, and frankly, too old, at sixty-one, to be playing it cool. The man had not laid a glove on me, and yet we'd had three great dates (if you leave out the music parts).

He called the next day to make another date, and I told him I was off to California for a week, first to the Golden Door Spa for a tune-up, then to Los Angeles—where I had not been since my Hollywood marriage ended. He asked to exchange email addresses, and so we emailed during the California trip. I was surprised at the warmth of his messages ("I really miss seeing you") and his wish to get together the day I returned, if that were possible.

My time at the Golden Door was a hoot, as were all my spa excursions. I never did any of the exercises. I read. For the fun of it, this time I tried a tap class, but being the only one who couldn't follow the directions, I felt deeply humiliated and was pretty sure these women had all gotten together in someone's room to practice without me. I guess I went to those places for a change of scenery, peace and quiet, and the 1,200 calories a day disguised as a feast by really talented chefs.

When I left there for LA it was to catch up with a few chums from my former life. One girlfriend, hearing about the doctor, asked if I thought it might be going anywhere. I actually did (even without a single goodnight kiss), so she took me to what she said was *the* most wonderful lingerie store. I had a hunch this man was still waters. There was definitely a spark between us, and I just assumed that when he felt the time was right, he would initiate the logical next step—ergo, I wanted to have a few new nightgowns made. One that I tried on was really gorgeous but rather complicated. I figured if I couldn't get into it, I couldn't get out of it, so I settled on a few simple, flowing numbers with spaghetti straps in gossamer floral prints. They would be sent when they were finished.

Knowing I was going to Los Angeles, a Cambridge friend set up a blind date for me. It was with the comedian Mort Sahl, of all people. I had seen him perform in Chicago years before and thought he must be one hundred years old. (In fact, he was then seventy.) But what a nice surprise he turned out to be. I expected a monologue for the whole night, but he wasn't "on" at all. We had a leisurely dinner with very good conversation, mostly about politics. And that was the last date I ever had with anyone who wasn't named Weintraub.

Given the doc's innate reserve, it seemed out of character that his emails conveyed such eagerness for me to return. Could we have dinner, he wrote, the day I got back? On his schedule was a straightforward afternoon case, so why didn't he come to me when he was finished and we could have take-out in the kitchen? Which is what we did.

Something in him had opened up, and the conversation continued with familiarity and ease. The subject of movies came up. He was a film enthusiast. I asked if he'd like to see the trailer for Adam's movie that would be shown out of competition at Cannes. And so we went upstairs to the den and I fished out Adam's DVD. We watched the snippet of film and then, in what I thought was an old-fashioned and adorable prelude, he said, "Let's neck." This was no goodnight kiss, and he was, as common parlance has it, a good kisser. And . . . we were necking, but it dawned on me that we were on a glove leather sofa.

"This thing is so smooth we could fall off and break something. Let's go downstairs where there's a suede sofa."

"Why don't we just lie down?" he suggested without hesitation.

"On what?" I said. "The floor?"

He said a bed would certainly be more comfortable. I couldn't argue with that, and thought that just because we were on a bed didn't mean we had to get in it. But about forty-five minutes later things had progressed, and he suggested we get *more* comfortable.

"That will not be possible. The UPS man hasn't come yet." I blurted.

"Wait, we need the UPS man?" he said, confused by this nonsequitor.

"Well, you see, I ordered nightgowns especially for this occasion, and they haven't been delivered yet."

He laughed. At that point I excused myself to use the loo and felt that even without my new lingerie the time was right, so I put on a Jean Harlow-esque satin number and returned to the bedroom. For decorum's sake I will end the narrative here, save for pointing out that this was our fourth date (my lucky number) and I couldn't help thinking, regarding no previous goodnight kisses, that this man did not believe in doing things by half measures. I also realized because there was such great chemistry between us (a surprise, I admit it), I had to acknowledge that maybe I didn't have a "type" at all.

Before I arrived on the scene, Ron had been going out with different women. He told me one criterion was that they be age-appropriate, having put a toe in the water of young nurses and finding it not particularly comfortable. This was an atypical attitude for someone of his age and accomplishment. His feeling about younger women was apparently Neil Simon's, who had remarked to friends, "They don't know the songs." Of course the doc immediately got points for this rather unusual resolve.

One early hurdle presented itself. We were seeing each other exclusively, both of us aware that this relationship was special and that it was working. He told me, however, that before we met he'd invited another woman he was seeing to accompany him to a surgical meeting in New Orleans. I asked him to tell me, in broad outline, who this woman was. He said she didn't particularly mean anything to him when he invited her, but that he'd wanted a date for this meeting. I found that problematic. My thinking was, and I told him, that we had embarked on something we both found to be meaningful, and the interruption would not be helpful. I asked what did he have to lose by clearing the playing field for one month? (That length of time was an arbitrary choice, but I did think that thirty days would be all that was necessary to close the deal.)

My reasoning prevailed and he said, with a twinkle, "Well, now you'll have to come to New Orleans." It was a lovely trip, incidentally, during which we learned we traveled well together. And that was the end of what's-her-name.

I knew in my gut where this was going. When I told friends about my doctor, once they heard he was a cardiac surgeon, more than one of them said, "Run. They are egomaniacs with God complexes, and you will become his scrub nurse." The strange thing was that although Ron was not without ego, he was an atypical CT surgeon. (Ironically, he often referred to himself as "a humble country doctor.") I was later to learn that he was a beloved mentor to the younger docs he trained and generous to colleagues, never overbearing or demanding. (I would go on to meet some of the "typical" Harvard heart surgeons, and then I understood what a gem—and an outlier—he was.) In fact, my name for him in the early days was "Dr. Pussycat."

It is a reality of a surgeon's life that there is limited time between cases. During these intermissions they either go to the doctors' lounge for coffee or stop at a nurses' station to look at emails until paged—at which time they split, usually without exiting whatever they were looking at on the computer. At a Beth Israel party one night a male nurse approached me and asked if he might ask a personal question. I said yes, thinking it couldn't be that personal.

"Is your name for Dr. Weintraub 'Dr. Pussycat'?"

I told him it was, and we laughed. He said he'd seen an email to him with that salutation on a computer at the nurses' station. When I told Ron, he said, "Thank you so much. Cardiac is considered the most macho of the surgical specialties, and now I am Dr. Pussycat." (Although I call him "Pussycat" to this day, I refer to him as "Dr. Perfect," out of deference to his macho sensibilities.)

I always felt there was an element of fate involved in our meeting. Putting all the coincidences together made it seem *bashert*— Yiddish for "meant to be." Consider: Ron's marriage to Sondra, ended by death after only two years, became a famous Harvard love story. Erich Segal was a year behind Ron at the College, and went on to write a book about the medical school. *Love Story* came out as a novel as well as a movie in 1970. I was Segal's date to the premiere of the movie—and Ken Howard had been seriously considered for the part that Ryan O'Neill ultimately got.

Ours was a successful yin and yang, the complementary version of "opposites attract"—far from the fire and ice I lived through with Coleman. By my lights Ron was on the quiet side, but when he spoke it was often to say something substantial. I on the other hand... And great good luck, he was entertained by me. Friends said that when I talked or told stories, you could see in his expression his affection for me. He knew I was the show, and it gave him pleasure.

Looking back, I am grateful I was mature enough not to lop it off with him after the first date "because he wasn't my type." I must have subconsciously factored in something my mother used to say: "You can dress them up or slim them down, but beyond that, forget it." Since he was beautifully tailored, I thought maybe he might lose some of the avuncular aspect (i.e., weight), which, in fact, he did go on to do without my having to say anything. Being able to get beyond the surface, or "type," if you will, made it possible for me to look for things that mattered. This is what prompted me, both in my advice column and when counseling friends, to always advise giving a new person a second look, as it is not possible to get a read on someone after just one encounter.

I had miraculously stumbled onto a grown-up. When I got to him, he had no demons, no "issues" he was still working out. This was a man who had gotten where he wanted to go, professionally, and was comfortable in his own skin. He also had integrity— a quality I'm embarrassed to admit I'd never really thought about in anyone with whom I was involved. He was just wired to do the right thing. While his love life had been rocky, my own pile of pebbles made that aspect less jarring to me and easier to understand.

As a much younger woman I remember regarding people who had married more than twice as being either flighty, sex maniacs, spoiled or nuts. Even today, if the subject comes up, most people will ask incredulously, "You've been married *how* many times?" It is just hard to understand if you've not experienced it. In practical terms, I have found that ending a marriage and moving on is emotionally not all that different from ending a serious relationship. The wild card about divorce is that it most often involves the legal system relative to children, money and possessions. But come to think of it, these days relationships without the legal aspect can also involve children, money and possessions. Oh, and pets.

Joyfully, after New Orleans we were a committed couple. With or without marriage was to be determined. I was deeply touched when he told me he "hadn't been this happy in thirty-five years." I loved the connection to Sondra, the wife with whom he associated love and happy times. She was in no way a ghost for me, as is sometimes the case when a beloved partner dies — though as Ron pointed out, that time in his life was decades in the distant past. I think we both felt really lucky.

Another odd twist of fate bolstered our confidence that this romance had sprung from maturity and good judgment. By a strange coincidence we had both been seeing the same shrink: Dr. Booster. I named him that because when I first went to him I said I was embarrassed to be back in therapy after a Freudian analysis, plus seeing a psychiatrist after that. He said I should just think of him as "a booster shot." However, I was a patient for four years, whereas Ron went to him three times, basically looking for some insight as to why he was making inappropriate choices in wives. He felt like an outlier because all but two of his closest friends from college, medical school, training, and hospital staffs were in long, stable marriages.

In any case, when we figured out we had the same shrink, we each booked an appointment with Dr. Booster to ask essentially the same thing: We realize you can't say too much, but, knowing us both, whatever you feel able to say would be appreciated. Dr. Booster told Ron about me, "What you see is what you get. There is no artifice." He told me that Ron would be a "perfectly appropriate companion" for me, and was highly regarded in medical circles. He further mentioned that he could give me all the "emotional elements" B.H. and my former husbands could not. (It tickled me that he never remotely came close to these words, but he really thought B.H. was a douchebag.) Ron and I both realized Dr. Booster had gone out on a limb, given the constraints of psychiatrists talking about patients, and we greatly appreciated it. Bumping into him quite a while after that, I thanked him for probably bending the rules. He said he had not said anything that wasn't true and was very happy for us.

To me, Love Among the Ruins is a gift, though one to be handled adroitly. A benefit of earlier, unsuccessful marriages is that, if you're awake, you are able to interpret what you're seeing in the rearview mirror. The advantage of cogent hindsight is understanding what's important, what's not, what can be tolerated, or what just might be the same song, second verse. With age comes change, and often, a mellowing. The doc and I have discussed the fact that no matchmaker would have ever put us together when we were younger, and we've acknowledged—as have other remarried couples I know—that we wouldn't have looked at each other twenty-five years ago. Middle-aged awareness and insight are not unlike the rock cycle (minus the million years required). Weather and water smooth the rock, just as self-knowledge and identifying weaknesses improve people. Integrating old lessons is what makes middle-aged marriages work.

My luck, Ron had a cadre of devoted friends who said, in essence, they didn't think he needed to get married again, but *should* that seem like a possibility, they were going to have to sign off on it. And so it was that I had various committees to work my way through. His medical partners, who knew a great deal about his private life, were perhaps the most protective. While his circle thought his second wife was a sweet person (but a poor choice), they really disliked the one that came after her. Going through all these look-over meetings felt not unlike passing inspection at a co-op board meeting. I knew what was going on, but the meetings were kind of fun because the response I was getting was affirmative.

One of Ron's partners, his first hire and longtime friend, happened to be married to a therapist, a woman whose opinion the department relied on before hiring any new surgeons. Now a good friend, she told me, much later on, that at first she and her husband thought I might be too flamboyant, too "LA" for Ron, but they had come to the conclusion that 1) if I had picked Cambridge as the place to live I was probably smarter than I looked, and 2) if I had chosen Ron, I was definitely smarter than I looked.

I made it through and received the approval of the committees, so we were good to go. I honestly think, after what he had been through, if his friends had said "don't do this," he would've listened. We were, oddly, a great match. (And he was in no way demanding, so I never became his scrub nurse.) We were soon living together, *chez moi*, which he referred to as Margo's Bed & Breakfast in the Heart of Harvard Square. He lightheartedly complained that he was living in his car. (That meant his white doctor coat was hanging on the hook in the backseat.) He would call the hospital page operator each night to give her the number where he could be reached. She probably thought he had two women on the string. (Such a thing was not unheard of. Just ask any page operator.)

One night a week he would stay at his place to pay bills, etc. Occasionally we would be together there, which I thought of as going to "the country house." It was in a development literally set in the woods. When we'd go there I would take what we called my "hooker bag," the few things one needs for an overnight. Many docs, by the way, lived in that development because it was within walking distance of the Harvard hospitals. (They could also ski to work, should the weather demand it.)

Everyone was asking me, "What does Eppie think?"

My answer was: "Think about it. A Jewish heart surgeon from Harvard? She loves him sight unseen."

From everything I'd been telling her, she was, in fact, over the moon. At about our five-month mark I thought they should meet. I called Mother to say we'd like to come to Chicago. Wonderful, she said. And I said I assumed we would stay with her, as the children and I always had. She did, after all, have a fifteen-room apartment and a staff. When she said, "I don't think so. You'll have more fun at the Ritz," I thought I'd misheard her. I asked why not with her? She said, "Because you're not married." *What?!* I was a thrice-married, fifty-seven-year-old retired *femme fatale* and my forward-thinking mother said we couldn't stay with her because we weren't married? Then I figured it out. She was seventy-nine and not without vanity; she typically slept until noon, then had breakfast, met her hairdresser in "the beauty parlor room" and was not going to see a man — especially a new man — until she was looking her best, which I must say was damned good.

Well, we did have more fun at the Ritz. This trip crossed my birthday, and gorgeous flowers were in the room with this card:

> *I did not know, when I was 3, that your birthday*
> *would be the most important day in my life. It*
> *was, you are. Love, R.*

And on the tray with a room service order was a square jeweler's box with this card:

> *Since you stole my heart, which was used and*
> *imperfect, please accept this brand new one.*
> *I love you.*

In the box was a gold and diamond heart. Still waters, indeed. For a guy who was only occasionally given to tender talk, he was doing quite well with the written kind, not to mention knowing how to make romantic arrangements and buy jewelry! He was in no way withholding, but neither was he demonstrative. And of course Mother loved him. Not to mention that a longtime dream of hers for me had come true. Finally, *a doctor.*

Even though we had not made a decision about marriage, we did know we would be together until the end of time. I knew this was Mr. Right #4, with or without benefit of clergy. Maybe when you're older and surer of what you need and want, such a decision feels organic. The pace of this romance was different than anything that had come before, and *he* was different from anyone I'd ever been with. Time had seasoned both of us.

Ron put his place on the market, and his next present was something for "us." He underwrote the re-do of my second floor to accommodate two offices, a larger bedroom and a double dressing room. During the heavy-duty construction we vacated to what I called our graduate student apartment. For six weeks we were living in 750 square feet and sleeping on a futon! We didn't have a lot of our clothes, or much of anything else, but we did not kill each other, which we took as a good sign.

Ours was an exceedingly comfortable relationship. Ron somehow had the knack of managing me. I knew that I had always been spoiled and a bit of a *grande dame* in training. For whatever reason, my outlook and expectations somehow dovetailed with this Jewish Yankee who was un-showy and solid. Having figured me out, he was selective about what information he shared. In that great Jewish tradition, I had the capacity to worry about almost anything. This aspect of our alliance reminded me of what I had heard about Alfred Lunt and Lynn Fontaine. Lunt was said to have been so protective of Fontaine that he kept World War II from her.

I am also a hypochondriac, so of course I loved having an in-house physician. More than once I have awakened him in the middle of the night asking that he take my pulse, and he's always a good sport about it. Holding two fingers to my wrist, waiting a respectable number of seconds, he tells me all is well and to go back to sleep. Moreover, when I would read about someone having a particular disease I would ask him what the symptoms were. His answer was always the same: "I'm not telling you."

Having no heart issues, save for a faint murmur, I pretty much fall outside his area of expertise. As we grow older I find myself wishing he were maybe an orthopod, a rheumatologist, a dermatologist, a psychiatrist or, at the very least, a gerontologist. I must say that when I was not somatizing or magnifying symptoms a hundred-fold, he was diligent about making the right arrangements. And you have not experienced VIP treatment until you are brought to the emergency room by a big deal surgeon who is on the staff.

My doc was certainly the most straight-laced man I had ever known, voicing astonishment that I could no longer remember all the names of the men I'd been involved with. In any case, he was the flying line to my kite. And we each enjoyed the other's world. He was stimulated by my intellectual and "literary friends," as he referred to both book writers and news people, and I found his group, many of them docs, to be smart, engaging and welcoming. There seemed to be something about that generation of physicians and surgeons—or maybe those from Harvard—that made for enviable, well-functioning first marriages.

There was a harmonic convergence in 1998 when we'd been together for a year. Ron encouraged me to go back to work at the same time I received an interesting offer. I'd already had a toy career in Boston that began and ended before I met him. When I'd been there for two years the new editor of *Boston Magazine*, Mike Roberts, called. He heard I was in town, and having bought my column when he was with the *Cleveland Plain Dealer*, he thought I should do a column for the magazine because I had new eyes on the city, just as he did. We worked out a column for me that would anchor the back of the book, calling it "Lunch on the Left Bank," an homage to the widely known nickname, "The People's Republic of Cambridge." I could select anyone I found interesting for a luncheon interview, and, as in Chicago, my questions were to be eccentric and offbeat, making for a non-standard portrait. I chose people like Kevin White and Derek Bok, who Bostonians certainly knew of but were never written about with a sense of fun. This lasted three years. Roberts left, the new editor kept me for a while, but then things petered out. Or as one friend said, hearing me talk about my tenure at *Boston Magazine*, "Margo, things did not 'peter out.' You were fired."

The doc got his wish when Michael Kinsley called and asked me to write an advice column for his newest undertaking, Slate.com. He had been my editor at the *New Republic*, and by my lights, the best magazine guy in the country. We had been friends for a long time. Of course he knew of my aversion to anything having to do with advice. I always felt that was the ol' lady's deal and it never interested me, though I'd had many offers through the years.

Mike led by acknowledging his understanding of my hiding from writing an advice column, *but* he thought he could change my mind. His selling points were as follows. First, it would be only four letters a week, divided into two days, not like my mother's seven columns a week. He knew this would be appealing because I was known in the business as someone low on ambition who never wanted to kill herself working. Second, I could make it anything I wanted. Finally, best of all, it would run online, and the copy could be transmitted by email. At that point I stopped him, asking if I could fax it in. Although I had a computer (to me, a newfangled typewriter), all I knew how to do was send emails to friends. I hadn't a clue how one would attach a separate document.

Then I told him I had no idea if I could even write an advice column. He said he was coming to Cambridge in a week, something to do with the law school, and he would come over and plug in my computer. We had a tutoring session. (My tutors would go on to include a young man who had washed our cars in California as a teenager who was now a muckety-muck with the National Security Agency. He was passing through Boston and asked to have dinner. I said yes—if he would give me a lesson. Future teachers followed: my internist's 14-year-old techie son, then my hairdresser's 12-year-old. I found the age regression telling…and now, of course, little kids have iPads.)

Mike explained that the originator of the Dear Prudence column had been Herb Stein (Nixon's economist!) who'd written it for a year before calling it quits. Herb had been anonymous, but I would not be. Mike sent me some letters, and I tried my hand at them, having decided I would not rely on experts, as my mother had. I would give reign to my humor, experience would be my guide, and I would be pragmatic, as opposed to politically correct.

Well, says she with no modesty, false or otherwise, I was a hit—and I had a feel for writing advice, this thing I had stayed away from for decades. I built Dear Prudence into one of Slate's big features, and it was actually great fun. Mother thought my columns were wonderful, as did her syndicate, which went on to syndicate my Prudie columns in two hundred newspapers.

I was later to write as Dear Margo when I left Slate for Yahoo! and I finally wound up at wowOwow.com, a women's site started by a group of accomplished middle-aged babes from the worlds of media and entertainment.

A thrice-divorced advice columnist, I grant you, could lead to a crisis of confidence for those seeking guidance. For whatever reason, that did not happen, and my marriages were accepted as a mere footnote. The fact that a colorful marital history did not invalidate my advisory voice may have been because divorce had become so common (most studies put the divorce rate at 50%). Perhaps in the same way that people believed an experienced Outward Bound instructor could keep them from falling out of a tree, readers accepted that I knew the ropes on the subject of marriage. The advice-giving community certainly is not, and was not meant to be, made up of perfect people with perfect lives (assuming they exist, which, alas, they do not). The advice columnist's work product really is *the* prime example of, "Don't do as I do, do as I say." So the doc got his wish, and I began yet another career, finally going into the family business.

Bill Gates was a generous overlord. We had yearly Slate retreats at lovely resorts a few hours outside of Bellevue in Washington State where upper-level tech and editorial people would meet for a long weekend. Depending on how you look at it, I was either the old bag of Slate or its *grande dame*. Most everyone was young. Kinsley, the founding editor, eleven years junior to me, was considered on the old side. I was as far from tech-savvy as they come, and at our first business session I was perplexed by all the discussion of the browser. Rather than continue to sit there with no idea of what they were talking about, I raised my hand and asked, "What is a browser?" There was disbelief and silence all around the table, until one of the tech people finally defined it for me in language that a seven-year-old could understand.

In time I figured it all out, and I was thrilled to be associated with Slate, which among its other attributes, was a reliable training ground for the *New York Times* and the *New Republic*.

It struck me as ironic that just as Ron had persuaded me to go back to work he was starting to plan his own exit. He'd been giving a great deal of thought to retiring. Careful as he was in all things, he took three years to make the final decision. (When we would go to national surgical society meetings he'd ask retired surgeons if they missed the action—and not one of them did.)

When I knew he would soon bring his thirty-five-year career in the operating room to an end, I decided that I wanted to see him at work, if only to understand a little of what his professional life had entailed. I had also never seen surgery performed. For me to do this, several permissions were needed, and I was allowed in as a journalist. The nurse in charge of me had the title of "circulating nurse." She was the only one on the "team" who could use the phone, talk to me, or interact with those in the sterile operating field if something was needed from outside the OR.

I knew the chief of anesthesiology socially, and it was he who was heading the anesthesia team for this operation. To be friendly, he invited me to stand with them and observe from behind the ether screen—a short metal divider that separated the operative field from the anesthesiologists. This would give me a view of the patient from behind her head looking at, and ultimately into, her chest.

Of course I had to be in scrubs. And then I got to see, first-hand, what I had only imagined—although in actuality it looked like what that setting always looked like on television: bright lights, trays of instruments, no windows. Ron was in scrubs, wearing clogs and operative loupes. (A younger surgeon he hired from Texas wore cowboy boots when he operated. Dealer's choice.) As they got organized, classical music started to play. No surprise whose choice that was—just a small example of the lead surgeon being the big dog, or God, with whom some of them confused themselves.

I was told the patient I would see that day was a Hispanic woman who needed a double valve replacement. As she was wheeled in on the gurney there was a frantic commotion just as the OR doors opened. The circulating told me the woman had "arrested" (experienced cardiac arrest) on her way into the OR! So instead of the usual organized procedures, what was going on was chest compression to resuscitate her *and* applying Betadine solution and drapes for surgery. The drape looked to me like blue-green butcher paper, under which the woman looked like she was wrapped in Saran wrap. That actually was transparent plastic that sticks to the skin and through which the incision is made.

The "opening" and "closing" in cardiac surgery, despite its theatrical sound, is opening the chest with (smelling salts, please) a saw, then suturing everything closed when the operation is finished. Ordinarily a junior surgeon might tend to this, but because of the woman arresting, Ron did it himself to save time. Well, to make a long operation short, I am peering into the open chest of a woman who is now orange (from Betadine) and after fifteen minutes I had seen enough of innards and blood and the human heart. I caught the eye of the circulating nurse and motioned with my head that I was leaving. I was later told that about an hour into the operation Ron noticed I wasn't there and asked if I were coming back. The nurse said she very much doubted it.

For whatever reason, the fact that the woman was orange was extremely unsettling to me. But then I remembered it could have been worse. And, years ago, it had been. When Ron was a house officer at the Mass General, he and another resident were left in charge one weekend when their chief was out of town. A patient suffering from liver disease had to be taken back to the OR because he was leaking lymphatic fluids. The lymphatic vessels are minuscule and their fluid is clear, making them almost impossible to spot. Ron, having been a "mouse doctor" at the National Institutes of Health (doing research on mice), thought if they used "vital blue" dye they would be able to spot the leaking vessels. He tried to do a computation of the amount of dye needed by multiplying the dosage for a mouse by a factor he felt would give him the desired result for a human. He then injected that amount of dye into the groin where it would be picked up by the lymphatics. A few minutes later he heard urgent whispering from the anesthesia people. Then one of them said, "Dr. Weintraub, something is very wrong." Apparently yellow jaundice and too much blue dye make green. I only knew about this because "the green man" story became famous at the General, and many of his old comrades in arms told me.

We'd now been together for three years—still unmarried—and a bad birthday was looming. My sixtieth freaked me out. I think zero-birthdays are bad for women. (It can't just be me.) Knowing of my distress, Ron offered me anything I wanted. What I wanted was to get out of Dodge. Neither of us had been to the South Pacific, so that would be our trip, and he proved to be a master planner. For one thing, we would be gone for five weeks because he said you couldn't properly see Australia and New Zealand on the fly. His partners were wide-eyed when he told them he'd be away for five weeks. No one in the department had ever been gone that long. I was wide-eyed because, in deference to my fear of wrong-side-of-the-road driving, Ron said he would hire a car and driver going from place to place when we were not flying. While the dear boy was not ungenerous, he was a Yankee, which I put somewhere between frugal and practical. I was neither. He did not know from extravagance until I taught him.

We started with four days in Fiji at Turtle Island, where we had a thatched-roof villa on a private beach. The place was gorgeous, restful and romantic. (Bonus trivia: it was where they filmed *The Blue Lagoon* with Brooke Shields.) My first birthday party (of three) was on another part of the island. We were driven there and parked ourselves oceanside under four tent poles holding a brightly colored canvas top. Shortly after our arrival—from the sea!—came a canoe with three Fijians wearing leis and singing "Happy Birthday." They unloaded our picnic lunch of lobster, Cloudy Bay Sauvignon Blanc, and a miniature birthday cake. They said the Jeep would return for us in three hours.

Leaving by seaplane, as we had arrived, we were delivered to Nadi airport for the flight to Sydney. There we stayed at the stupendous Park Hyatt in the Rocks district, facing the famous opera house that looked as though it could fly away at any minute. I had the feeling in Sydney that if I were younger, it might've been a perfect place to live. It was like the United States fifty years ago—in the good way. And there were so many different climates, all in the same country! The doc went hiking; I did not.

We went to other cities that were less cosmopolitan but no less wonderful. My second birthday party was in Canberra, where we were the houseguests of a spook Ron had met during an Advanced Management Program course he'd taken at Harvard Business School. He knew I knew what he did for his government, so one morning when he and Ron went out walking, he told me I was free to use his computer but to please be careful not to start any wars.

We went with him for two days to his rustic beach house... somewhere. The water of the Tasman Sea and the trees were truly breathtaking, as were the stunningly colored birds, many of which were to be seen nowhere else in the world. Their wild-flowers are considered a protected species so you may not pick them—though I saw no gendarmerie lurking around. Our host had a bag of birdseed, which he threw on the picnic table in front of the house, saying, "Watch this!" It took about six seconds for great numbers of birds to materialize from everywhere. I felt like Tippi Hedren in *The Birds*.

Everything was wonderful but for the small fact that there was no indoor plumbing. I tried really hard to be a good sport about it, even though when I heard this news I wanted to throw *myself* on the barbie. You cannot imagine what courage it took for me to lightly push a kangaroo aside who seemed to want to go into the little outhouse with me. I was to learn I was fortunate in that the roo I got assertive with was young, because I later read of a grown-up one who'd beaten a twelve-year-old boy to death with his tail. Oh, God, I thought. As if it weren't bad enough to have to use an outhouse in the first place, to breathe your last because a marsupial was wrestling you for the privilege was beyond the pale.

Our last stop in Australia was Melbourne, which struck me as a lot like Chicago, while Sydney felt more like the Aussie New York. Then on to New Zealand, considered Australia's younger, less sophisticated sibling, but I loved it. Have you ever seen thousands of reindeer and sheep on acres and acres of gorgeous land? My third and final birthday party was in Wellington with yet another spook from Harvard Business School. Three birthday parties and five weeks later, I was properly sixty and quite chipper about it.

A year after the dreaded zero birthday, in 2001 we celebrated four years of unwedded bliss. For this anniversary Ron wanted to try a new restaurant after I attended the opening of something or other on Newbury Street. When he collected me after the cocktail party launch he said he was feeling a little off, and asked if we could we skip the new restaurant and just go home and have some soup. We got home, opened the front door, and all the lights were low. We were greeted by an attractive young woman in a ladies' tux, and the small round table by a glass wall of windows was set with china, silver, and lit candles. The most marvelous catered dinner was served, with champagne. For dessert, along with something sweet (I am not sentimental or young enough to remember the menu), there was a small, wrapped, oblong package, maybe five inches long—obviously not a ring. (The dear boy was smart enough to know I had a surplus of those.) I opened the wrapping and then the velvety jeweler's box to see a large diamond-studded gold pin. I was greatly touched when I interpreted its meaning. Framed inside an abstract heart, representing his life's work, was a quill, symbolizing mine, and three larger diamond eighth notes denoting his love of music. Engraved on the back was the legend, "Grow old along with me, The best is yet to be. Ron, 2001." He had rustled up a custom jeweler and directed the design. Our official engagement was confirmation that this not terribly demonstrative man was, indeed, still waters and a closet romantic in the bargain.

As we went forward making a life together he graciously came to terms with the fact that I was never going to be his companion on the slopes. (Though I did like some of the lodges and acquired quite an après ski wardrobe. I accompanied him on numerous ski trips—his favorite being the Alta Lodge in Utah, don't ask me why. There were no phones in the room, no TVs, and it struck me as a Motel 6 with snow. After a short while I worked it out that the guests, some famous, many rich, were Aspen-averse, hence the ultra simplicity.)

He also made his peace with the fact that I did not like opera or choral music, so I was excused from some of his concert evenings. He was an exceptionally good sport about the fact that I read during symphony performances—I found it odd that people just sat there and listened, doing nothing—but the ground rule was that I could not make any rustling paper noises, so I would tear out pages of articles I wanted to read. His seats were mercifully under lighting that was adequate to read by. It just seemed a waste not to be able to read with all that beautiful background music. I had tried to tell him, early on, that I was rather uncultured, but I don't think he believed me. With time, however, he agreed that I was, indeed, as he elegantly put it, "a fucking Philistine."

The question of whether or not we would marry was answered by sad circumstance. When my mother was diagnosed, at age eighty-three with terminal multiple myeloma, I felt, and Ron agreed, that our getting married would bring her comfort. She would go more peacefully knowing I was being looked after by a grown-up. We were married in our living room on December 23, 2001 by Ron's longtime rabbi, Bob Miller, with his wife as a witness. By the Rabbi's instruction, Ron wrapped a light bulb in a dish towel so he could step on it, thereby "breaking the glass" of traditional Jewish weddings. We spoke our own vows to each other and the whole deal took maybe ten minutes. I wore black slacks and a sweater, on which, of course, was the engagement pin. Then we four went to dinner. That was it. Truly, this was such a non-event that we made no announcement. I casually mentioned it, a few months later, in my "Dear Margo" column in response to a question about remarriage, and for quite a long time people would ask us if we were married or still just livin' in sin. The person who needed to know did know, and she died six months later on June 22, 2002.

At age sixty-five Ron hung up his scalpel. Having operated for thirty-five years, he wanted to quit while, in his mind, he was still a good surgeon. He did not want to lose facility, and felt ready to off-load the tension attached to thinking about his patients from yesterday, today, and the ones tomorrow. He believed that more than a few surgeons stayed too long at the fair. There was one whose nickname was "Shaky Jake." This is true.

His plans for retirement were to take courses at Harvard, become expert at photography, and travel more. None of these things happened. The White Coat Brigade conspired to keep him in the game — though not in scrubs. The chief of surgery at the merged Beth Israel Deaconess Medical Center was on the search committee for a chief of surgery at the Cambridge Health Alliance, a trio of Harvard-affiliated safety-net hospitals. This doc was an old friend and admirer of Ron's, as was the chief of medicine at CHA. Together, they convinced him to become interim chief of surgery and rebuild the department. It was felt that his technical and people skills could return credibility to a department in need of guidance. Ron thought retirement could be put off for six months, so he agreed. After six months, however, they asked him to become the chief of surgery — no more interim. His condition was that he participate in the choice of his replacement, believing that a non-operating chief wasn't in the best interests of the institution.

He asked if I would mind. I thought a second career that came as a surprise was wonderful. Redoing the department and hiring younger surgeons, as well as a new chief, took three years. His thank you to me for "letting him" be chief was a Cartier watch I hankered after. The only way he could have known I had my eye on that particular watch must have been the pictures of it that somehow landed on his desk at regular intervals. (Lest you think his language of love was restricted to gold and diamonds, my favorite foods were also in his repertoire. When he would come home with kumquats, figs, avocados, or mangoes, I knew he was saying I love you, with the help of Whole Foods.) So, after three years he hired the new CHA chief of surgery and was *really* planning to retire. Curses. Foiled again. They found ways to hang on to him by putting him on committees and making him the surgical safety officer. I took great pride in the fact that he was as beloved there as he had been at the Beth Israel.

We were known everywhere, and traveled as Dr. Weintraub and Mrs. Howard. I did not change my name after the divorce because Margo Howard had been a professional name for a very long time. And it was funny about that name and Cambridge, a place aggressively not knowledgeable about Hollywood. (The exception: when a movie was shot there.) Ron Howard and Ken Howard were often confused because of having the same last name, with their first names being only three letters and ending in the same consonant. It got to the point where people would say to me whenever Ron Howard had a success (which was often and well publicized, as he is an important producer and director with his own production company), "Wonderful about your ex-husband's triumph!" I always figured it was just easier to say "Thank you." (Apologies to Ron Howard and his longtime and only wife, Cheryl.)

I realized, relative to Dr. Perfect's career, that I had been with each husband during the best time of his life. This had nothing to do with me; you cannot plan these things, after all. But consider: During the time the Starter Husband and I were married he became wealthy, and, let us say for legal reasons as well as those of *politesse*, less "eccentric" than he went on to become. (Mr. Right #2 might be exempt from this calculation because the marriage was so short I don't really know *what* the best time of his life was.) Mr. Right #3 was most famous and flush during our years together; and Dr. Perfect had all the demanding career-building years behind him long before I came on the scene.

I must say, in the milestone department, it was a lovely feeling for both Ron and me to turn seventy with a beloved spouse. For his seventieth I rented a villa outside of Florence and invited six couples for a house party. It was a splendid week—and distinctive. (For instance, our Tamil butler wore a T-shirt.) After breakfast each day some couples would go on excursions, others would hang around swimming or reading. Dinner was all of us, "a casa" or in a restaurant. We had a terrific cook, but she didn't speak English! Great good luck, a girlfriend on the trip was an Italian speaker, so we were able to plan menus without inadvertently requesting door knobs in glue sauce.

Four years later, to get me through *my* seventieth, the doc chartered a barge and invited three couples of my nearest and dearest to celebrate with us on a trip through Burgundy. I don't know how you say it—we barged through Burgundy?—but the pace is truly slow; slow enough that some of us could jog or bicycle faster than the canal boat. The van that took us from Paris to the boat followed us on the road for day trips, and to take us to one evening outing at a three-star restaurant where, surprisingly to me, they sold a book about the founding chef's suicide! We had five crew with us, and our chef was as good as the one at the three-star. Lunches and dinners on board always offered different wines and many cheeses with the fine French food. It was both divine and *de trop*. Seven days later the trip was over and we were driven to Paris. Four of us went out for a hamburger.

After the two birthday parties in Europe we decided birthday celebrations were *finis*. It just felt better to ignore them. Aging, of course, is on one's mind after achieving the three score and ten mentioned first in the Bible, then in Macbeth. Age and health figure prominently in life after seventy, so of course many of us talk about it. My mother's name for that was having an "organ recital." (She, herself, however, never discussed the subject, and took the position that "How are you?" was a greeting, not a question.) The seventy-plus crowd that we know both talk about it, and laugh. It is no accident that the archaic meaning of "humor" was anything related to bodily fluids having to do with sickness.

Of course young marrieds are not exempt, but one thing late-life couples can expect to get, besides Social Security, is sick. Considering what *can* happen, however, the doctor and I have been lucky in requiring, between us, only back surgery, foot surgery, hand surgery, stents, and treatment for the stones: gall and kidney. All the aging crap is hardly worth the senior discounts, but, as far as I know, it was never an either/or situation. Benefits of "the golden years" aside, nobody is thrilled about getting older. Your parts wear out, rust, need replacement or patching up. The redeeming feature of advancing decrepitude, however, is sharing it with a partner you love. I am profoundly grateful to be growing old with Dr. Perfect. He was worth the wait.

ACKNOWLEDGMENTS

Heartfelt thanks to Mark Feeney, for badgering me to just sit down and do it. And to Alice Arlen, who repeated the instruction.

To longtime friend, Ike Williams, agent *extraordinaire,* and his sidekick, Katherine Flynn, for invaluable advice and tireless efforts.

To Deb Brody and her gang of girl warriors at Harlequin. Deb's was the steady hand guiding me, a hand that often had a red pencil in it, to be sure, but a finer editor a girl could not have. And to publicity director Shara Alexander, and the team in Toronto (with a special shout out to the designers who actually considered my idea for the cover art and went with it!).

To good and dear writer friends who were early readers and wildly generous in their enthusiasm: Rebecca Goldstein, the late Roger Ebert, Mike Kinsley, and Kitty Kelley.

To Anne Peretz, a close friend for almost five decades, who sat in her therapist's chair to give me the prism through which to view my past.

To Dr. Booster, who knew where I should be, and helped me get there. To the husbands who made my monogram—MPLCFHW—really impressive.

To the memory of my mother, who was a peach about all the husbands coming and going.

Of course, special love to my doc, who outlasted them all.